LINCOLN CHRISTIAN UNIVERSITY
LANGUAGE AND LITERACY SERIES
Dorothy S. Strickland, FOUNDING EDITOR
Celia Genishi and Donna E. Alvermann, SERIES EDITORS

ADVISORY BOARD: Richard Allington, Kathryn Au, Bernice Cullinan, Colette Daiute, Anne Haas Dyson, Carole Edelsky, Shirley Brice Heath, Connie Juel,

(Continued)

For volumes in the NCRLL Collection (edited by JoBeth Allen and Donna E. Alvermann) and the Practitioners Bookshelf Series
(edited by Celia Genishi and Donna E. Alvermann), please visit www.tcpress.com.

THE SUCCESSFUL HIGH SCHOOL WRITING CENTER

Building the Best Program with Your Students

Edited by

Dawn Fels

Jennifer Wells

Foreword by Richard Kent

Teachers College, Columbia University
New York and London

National Writing Project
Berkeley, California

Published simultaneously by Teachers College Press, 1234 Amsterdam Avenue, New York, NY 10027 and National Writing Project, 2105 Bancroft Way, Berkeley, CA 94720-1042.

The National Writing Project (NWP) is a professional development network of 200 university-based sites, serving teachers across disciplines and at all levels, early childhood through university. The sites work in partnership with surrounding school districts across all 50 states, the District of Columbia, Puerto Rico, and the U.S. Virgin Islands. The NWP focuses the knowledge, expertise, and leadership of our nation's educators on sustained efforts to improve writing and learning for all learners.

Library of Congress Cataloging-in-Publication Data

The successful high school writing center : building the best program with your
    students / edited by Dawn Fels, Jennifer Wells ; foreword by Richard Kent.
        p. cm. — (Language and literacy series)
    Includes bibliographical references and index.
    ISBN 978-0-8077-5252-4 (pbk. : alk. paper)
    ISBN 978-0-8077-5253-1 (alk. paper)
        1. English language—Rhetoric—Study and teaching. 2. Report writing—Study
    and teaching. 3. Creative writing (Higher education) 4. Writing centers. 5. Tutors
    and tutoring. I. Fels, Dawn. II. Wells, Jennifer, 1977–
    PE1404.S853 2011
    808'.042071273--dc23   2011017768

ISBN 978-0-8077-5252-4 (paper)
ISBN 978-0-8077-5253-1 (hardcover)

Printed on acid-free paper
Manufactured in the United States of America

18   17   16   15   14   13   12   11   8   7   6   5   4   3   2   1

DEDICATIONS

Dawn Fels

In loving memory of my mother, Eileen "Lynn" Tipton, who taught me how to appreciate literacy and good stories. For my high school English teacher Mary Wille, who taught me how to write and to advocate for students. And to my children, Cameron and Zada, who teach me about love and life.

Jennifer Wells

To my dad, Byron Wells, who taught me how to ask questions and really listen, and whose love has not been conquered by death, and to my mom, Suzanne Wells, who for 41 years changed the lives of her students, one-to-one.

Contents

Foreword

American education will never realize its potential as an engine of opportunity and economic growth until a writing revolution puts language and communication in their proper place in the classroom. Writing is how students connect the dots in their knowledge.
—*The Neglected "R": The Need for a Writing Revolution,* Report to Congress National Commission on Writing, 2003

During the first decade of the 21st century, the National Writing Project, National Council of Teachers of English, and National Commission on Writing called for a renewed emphasis on writing and advocated for a writing revolution. If an uprising in the world of writing is needed—as many of us believe it is—there are no more qualified activists and leaders than Dawn Fels and Jennifer Wells, writing center practitioner-scholars and co-editors of this book.

My first connection with Dawn's work took place at the 2004 National Council of Teachers of English Convention in Indianapolis. During one session of her workshop on secondary school writing centers, Dawn spoke about the disenfranchised student-writers at her urban-suburban high school in a school district where 70% of the student population received free or reduced-price lunch. In seamless fashion, Dawn "connected the dots" of her writing center work to the foundational theories of writing and learning. At the time, I remember thinking how my own writing center experiences would have been enhanced (and more joyous) had Dawn been my colleague when I was a fledgling director.

In 2010, those of us in the high school writing center world celebrated Dawn's doctoral dissertation. Dr. Fels's research topic, not surprisingly, relies on the narratives of writing center tutors. Her study adds students' perspectives to our profession's discussions of the effects of standardized writing instruction and assessment on teaching and learning. And much to my delight and benefit, Dawn and I have become long-distance colleagues in this rapidly growing secondary school writing center community.

In 2006, I led a workshop in New York City at the National Writing Project's annual meeting. The session, titled "Creating Student-Staffed Writing Centers," filled eight round tables with high school teachers, college professors, pre-service teachers, writing-project leaders, high school students, and one galvanic, always-smiling writing center director who, as a non-participant in the writing project, crashed the gig. Actually, in an email exchange I had encouraged Jennifer Wells to join the workshop, and those in attendance were glad I did. Jenn illuminated our discussions by unpacking our understanding of a writing center's potential for a school while also showcasing the impact on tutors and clients.

With unbounded energy, Jenn serves on the boards of both the International Writing Centers Association and the Northern California Writing Centers Association. She collaborates with the National Writing Project, participating as a valued teacher-consultant, and contributes to the Conference on College Composition. Her 2008 award-winning *English Journal* article, "'It Sounds Like Me': Using Creative Nonfiction to Teach College Admissions Essays," showcased writing center work and is featured on the National Writing Project's resource website. Jenn's own high school reading and writing center has become a nationwide model. Now in the dissertation stage of her doctorate, Jenn will focus her study on how students transfer knowledge of reading and writing from high school to college.

Clearly, we readers could not be in more capable hands than those of Dawn Fels and Jennifer Wells. For this book, they have invited top-notch writing center practitioners and tutors from high schools and colleges. Wise and inventive, these collaborators share a wide range of firsthand knowledge while crafting a vision and a promise through snapshots of today's most important writing center collaborations and models.

As a result, the writing center world welcomes *The Successful High School Writing Center*, a book that holds transformational power. It is an immediately useful book, yes, but also a critical collection imbued with theory-to-practice models that address our marginalized students and their teachers.

Why writing centers? And how to even begin such a project? Two of the brightest stars in the 21st-century high school writing center world and their colleagues are about to help you find out.

—Richard Kent, University of Maine, October 2010
Author of *A Guide to Creating Student-Staffed Writing Centers, Grades 6–12*, winner of the Outstanding Book Award, 2006, from the International Writing Centers Association

REFERENCES

National Commission on Writing In America's Schools and Colleges. (2003). *The neglected "r": The need for a writing revolution.* Retrieved from http://www.collegeboard.com/prod_downloads/writingcom/neglectedr.pdf

Introduction

Dawn Fels and Jennifer Wells

Writing centers in U.S. high schools have existed since the late 1970s (Farrell, 1989); however, they have done so by flying under the radar. Up until recently, it was hard to argue against the skeptic who dismissed notions of teachers running writing centers in high schools. "Who in a high school could run a writing center?" is a question we have both been asked by those who did not know that they've existed for nearly 4 decades.

For various reasons, this question still comes up. Writing centers are often marginalized in the post-secondary composition community. They are even more marginalized in high schools, where they are not expected. This is especially true in high schools placed on corrective action, high schools that are underfunded, and high schools that serve diverse or marginalized student populations. Another reason is that many high school writing center directors are also full-time high school faculty with neither time nor incentive to publish their experiences or to present at conferences.

The Successful High School Writing Center: Building the Best Program with Your Students offers high school teachers, teacher educators, and university writing center directors both theoretical and practical information they can use to create and sustain writing centers in secondary schools. This collection brings readers the expertise of current and former high school writing center directors, as well as university collaborators who share stories of how they created their programs. The fact that each author enthusiastically contributed to this book while balancing a demanding job, doctoral studies, or both is testimony to their unwavering belief in the power of writing centers to effect systemic change in literacy education in secondary schools. This collection brings their stories from the margins to a wider audience of readers who may now join in their efforts to increase high school writing centers' presence in local communities, in the writing center field, and in related literacy education fields. Our contributors, then, model the potential of teacher-leaders to create and direct high school writing centers and increase awareness of their benefits to teaching and learning. After reading this book, it is our hope that readers will embrace writing centers as literacy leaders in all school communities, not just in those served by well-funded public or private schools.

Our contributors prove that not only do high school writing centers exist but also thrive in larger numbers than many would have anticipated. Each year, more and more high school writing center directors attend their first International Writing Centers Association (IWCA) conference. More and more attend sessions or all-day workshops sponsored by the IWCA at the annual convention of the National Council of Teachers of English (NCTE). More newcomers attend their first Conference on College Composition and Communication (CCCC) convention. We also see an increase in the number of university writing center directors and teacher-educators who collaborate with teachers to set up writing centers in area schools.

The growing interest in high school writing centers comes at a time when there is both a renewed emphasis on reading and writing instruction and a greater need to put teaching and learning back into the hands of teachers and students. In her 2007 address to attendees of the Midwest Writing Centers Association, Kathleen Blake Yancey described writing centers as the one site to which students return time and again throughout their school careers to learn critical and multiple literacy skills. The high school writing centers featured in *The Successful High School Writing Center* serve this necessary function for students while providing them with differentiated and individualized literacy instruction. But they also serve teachers through professional development programs, creative collaborative projects, and outreach to pre-service teacher education programs. These hallmarks of high school writing center work have led many to realize that high school writing centers are the ideal place to meet the needs of both students and teachers.

This book is organized to provide readers with a foundation in both theoretical and practical content about the various ways in which high school writing centers serve literacy education efforts in schools. Each author's story comes from his or her own experience working in or with secondary schools. For that reason, where necessary, the names of contributors' colleagues, tutors, and students have been changed to protect their identities.

In Chapter 1, "The Promise of Change With One-to-One Instruction," writing center scholar Ben Rafoth, who has practiced one-to-one writing center pedagogy for over 2 decades, joins us to lay the foundation for writing center work with a brief discussion of the main theories that underlie writing center pedagogy.

In Chapter 2, "Change I Can See: A High School English Teacher's Perspective of the Writing Center's Impact on Bilingual, Hispanic Students," high school teacher Katherine Palacio and her university collaborator Kevin Dvorak describe the effects of the writing center they created at a predominantly Hispanic high school on teachers, students, and students' families. Katherine outlines the steps she took to start the center with Kevin and his tutors from St. Thomas University and moves to a discussion of how she sustains the center through her own site-based research and communication with parents.

In Chapter 3, "The Idea of a High School Writing Center," Kerri Mulqueen, who created a writing center in a diverse Brooklyn high school, traces how her own experience as a graduate student tutor under the venerable Steven North affected her work as a teacher and writing center director. Kerri's chapter shows why the diversity among tutors should reflect the diversity of the student body and how students with diverse backgrounds (racial, academic, and linguistic) make great tutors and leaders among the student body. She also illustrates the reciprocal benefits of a peer tutoring program for students and tutors alike.

In Chapter 4, "Building a Peer Tutoring Program," Andrew Jeter provides readers with a thorough look at how he built what is inarguably the largest peer tutoring program in the country. He describes what it takes to manage his high school's extraordinary literacy center, which employs more than 200 peer tutors who log an astounding 30,000 or more sessions per year with students across disciplines. Perhaps more impressive than those numbers is Andrew's careful explanation of tutor training and appreciation programs that he and his staff created for tutors. The programs not only evolved from staying close to the center's mission but paying close attention to teenagers' learning styles, affect, and interests.

In Chapter 5, "Revising and Rewriting Roles: Exploring the Challenges of Peer Tutors in a High School Writing Center," Cynthia Dean shares findings from her study into how her high school's peer tutors negotiated their new roles with students and teachers. What's more, Cynthia set out to find specific ways in which tutors' identities were affected by their dual status as tutor and student. Her chapter includes the insights of many of her tutors whose expertise, professionalism, and reflection point to tutors' abilities to evaluate their role in the classroom and writing center.

We then celebrate the contribution of peer tutors to writing centers' efficacy and, consequently, students' success in Chapter 6, "The Tutors Speak: Current and Former Tutors' Reflections." This chapter, written and arranged by current and former peer tutors, brings together tutors' voices in a celebration of the benefits of writing centers to schools, students, and tutors. Following those tutors' observations are the reflections of three former high school writing center tutors—a filmmaker, a musician, and a teacher. Each traces how their writing center experiences followed them to college and graduate school and continue to influence them in their respective vocations. They prove that the benefits of a peer tutor program reach far beyond a student's high school tenure.

In Chapter 7, Jennifer Wells, a reading and writing specialist and founder of a writing center in an all-girls parochial high school, describes why high school writing centers are uniquely positioned to respond to the literacy crisis in a proactive way. The chapter, "Integrating Reading into the High School Writing Center," offers a theoretical and practical discussion of how writing centers are also reading centers and why, under the current *literacy crisis* that pervades schools across the country, many high school writing center directors are discovering the power of the center to support adolescent readers in both reading across the curriculum and for pleasure. She also describes the hybrid role of a literacy coach who is also a writing center director, and what such a combined writing/reading center can look like.

Jill Adams frames the success of a high school–university collaboration in Chapter 8, "Connecting Pre-Service Teachers with High School Writers," by showing how she and her pre-service teachers set up a writing center at a nearby school placed on corrective action. The program not only served as a writing center for the high school but also as a practice field for pre-service teachers to work one-to-one with students who struggled academically. As Jill's pre-service teachers' reflections show, the experience provided them with much more than they imagined possible.

Finally, in Chapter 9, "What State Auditors Taught Me About Writing Center Evaluation," Dawn Fels looks at writing center evaluation through the lens of a former high school writing center director and English teacher in a school of concern. She traces how conversations with state auditors over a 3-year period led her toward a more authentic assessment of writing center efficacy, an evaluation plan tied to the core values of the writing center's mission and the needs of teachers and students. Furthermore, the chapter offers models for how the writing center can lead literacy education efforts by providing professional and instructional support to teachers and students and celebrating achievements across the school community.

The book closes with helpful forms and projects that writing center directors can use to manage and assess their work. Each contributor also offers brief but helpful advice on how to negotiate various challenges known to arise when setting up or sustaining a center.

The Successful High School Writing Center provides aspiring and veteran writing center directors with models of writing centers that showcase individual and collaborative efforts. We've added new voices to the conversations about how secondary school writing centers help school communities grapple with the realities that come with literacy education. High school writing centers are not one-size-fits-all, nor should they be, and our contributors significantly expand the scholarship on high school writing centers by showcasing the writing center's diversity in real-life settings. By showing how high school writing centers can lead literacy education efforts, each contributor's story enriches the secondary education, writing center, and composition fields in socially significant and meaningful ways.

We are deeply indebted to our contributors. Their constant and enthusiastic devotion to students' literacy learning is evident in each chapter. We also want to acknowledge that for many, this book is their first publication, and we are honored to bring their voices to what has become an international conversation about how writing centers and literacy centers can best serve K–12 school communities. We'd also like to thank those who have supported our work as teachers and writing center directors over the years, starting with too many individuals to name who, through their work with the IWCA or National Writing Project (and in some cases, both), support high school writing centers in myriad ways. Among them are Pam Childers and Jeanette Jordan. Pam and Jenny welcomed us to the writing center field, and it was their tireless support of newcomers that inspired us to build this book around new voices in the field. We'd like to thank Amber Jensen for tirelessly promoting K–12 writing centers and for encouraging her tutors to submit reflections to this collection. Kathleen Blake Yancey offered her feedback on a very early (and rough) draft of our proposal; we owe her an uninterrupted tour of the Kansas City Art Museum. We would also like to thank Rich Kent for supporting this book from as early as the idea stage and for contributing the Foreword. Rich's advocacy of writing and literacy centers, of teachers, and of peer tutoring programs in K–12 schools is abundantly apparent in every aspect of his work. We thank him for working with us during his sabbatical, for his quick responses to emails, and for cheering us on from day one. We'd also like to thank Ben Rafoth, in whose office the idea for this book began to take shape. Ben has mentored and prepared more K–college educators for their dual roles in writing classrooms and writing centers than anyone else we know in the field, and we are among them. For his unwavering faith in us and this book, we thank him. And finally, we would like to acknowledge our colleague and friend John Tinker and his influence on this book. John introduced us at the IWCA's 2005 conference in Minneapolis. Both of us were avid fans of John's work at Stanford University with K–12 schools in Northern California, and we were honored when he agreed to contribute a chapter about Ravenswood Writes, a remarkable literacy program that supports literacy development in local public schools through the creation of writing centers. Sadly, shortly after our contributors began to work, John needed to step away from the project to focus on his health. His death leaves a huge void in this book, but more important, in both the education and writing center fields, where we know that John's devoted advocacy of K–12 writing centers will continue to inspire others.

This book's development is due in part to the careful review and feedback of our editors and reviewers at Teachers College Press. We'd like to thank our

Acquisitions Editor Meg Lemke and Development Editor Adee Braun. Since the day we first approached Meg with our idea for a book about high school writing centers, she has responded with nothing but support and encouragement. Her trust that we and our contributors would deliver what we promised provided a constant source of assurance, which was so important to those of us whose work is being published for the first time. Our thanks to Adee Braun for her quick, careful, and helpful feedback and insight into how this book might be useful for readers. Finally, we'd like to thank the anonymous reviewers for their positive, enthusiastic endorsement of our book. Not only did they agree that educators have waited long enough for a book about high school writing centers that served diverse student populations, but they provided helpful guidance on how to proceed with its development.

We'd each like to thank those closer to home whose collegiality, friendship, love, support, and sacrifice saw us through.

Dawn

I would like to thank my children, Cameron and Zada, for cheering me on, for asking questions about my work, and for weighing in on the ideas or portions of drafts that I shared with them. Their insights reinforced my conviction that if we really want to know the effects of teaching on students, we need only ask them. I would also like to thank my colleagues at Indiana University of Pennsylvania, especially Mike Williamson, Gian Pagnucci, and Gloria Park, as well as writing center director friends across the country, especially Brian Fallon, who celebrated the book's progress with announcements on listservs, high-fives in the hallways, and enthusiastic support on Facebook. (Yes, teachers use Facebook, too.) I owe a great deal to Cassie Luther, Trina Muniz, and Kerry Galeaz for keeping me grounded. And to my good friend and running buddy Marjie Stewart for teaching me how to take on the hills.

Jenn

I would like to thank my colleagues at Mercy High School for supporting the Reading and Writing Center with their words and actions, as well as my students at Mercy, especially the Writing Studies class, for being up for the adventure. I would also like to thank Randy VanderMey at Westmont College, Michael Mangin at Cabrillo College, Brian Kitely and Bin Ramke at the University of Denver, and Nelson Graff and Mark Roberge at San Francisco State, all of whom made an impact on me when I was their student. I am grateful to Zeph Harben for providing his shoulder, ear, and heart and for allowing me to do the same for him; Erika Yawger and Stephanie Quay for their unfailing support of all my crazy ideas; and, finally, my family, for everything.

CHAPTER ONE

The Promise of Change with One-to-One Instruction

Ben Rafoth, Jennifer Wells, and Dawn Fels

We would like to begin with the true story (Johnson, 2006) of two individuals living and working in the Soho neighborhood of London in the 1850s, one a doctor and the other a clergyman. But first, some background. Cholera is a dreadful waterborne disease that kills by dehydration within hours or days unless treated. Today, more than 6,000 people, mostly in Africa but also recently in Haiti, die every year from this preventable disease. One hundred sixty years ago in crowded, dirty, industrial London there were far-fetched beliefs about what caused cholera. Some believed that getting the disease depended on how close you were to the filthy, stinking streets, and so people who lived in first-floor or basement apartments were thought to be the most vulnerable. It wasn't true, but it meant you could rent a first-floor flat cheaper than one on a higher floor. Some believed that poor people were prone to the disease and the rich were not. By the middle of the 19th century, supposedly preventative measures and cures had been tried, but none worked. It was not until a doctor by the name of John Snow tried to see things from a different perspective that Londoners and the rest of the world learned how to stop the spread of contagion and save the community from devastation.

Widely considered to be the founder of modern epidemiology, Snow was a brilliant analyst who received considerable help from someone who, for a long time, resisted his perspective. The Rev. Henry Whitehead firmly believed the disease was caused by "bad air," but he would eventually yield to Snow's conclusion. Whitehead went house to house and spoke directly to the people still living there, gathering information that undermined his own notion and proved Snow's theory to be the correct one.

The puzzle began to fall into place when Snow created a unique street map that showed how many deaths had occurred at each address in the neighborhood. For every death at each address along every street in the neighborhood, Snow placed a hash mark on the map. This made it possible for Snow to see a pattern, and the pattern showed that the incidents of death seemed to radiate outward from one location on Broad Street. That location, known as the Broad Street pump, was also the place where the locals obtained their drinking water. The pump was not suspected of causing the outbreak. In fact, the Broad Street pump water was clear and known for its cool, fresh taste. Going house to house, Snow, Whitehead, and city officials asked questions about what the victims had eaten, where they had been before they fell ill, what remedies they had tried to ward off the disease, and where they had obtained their drinking water. Answers to the last inquiry proved key. Snow and Whitehead matched the pattern of the incidents of death to the source of the victims' drinking water—the Broad Street pump—and convinced the city council to remove the pump handle. It was a controversial decision, but when the number of deaths fell precipitously after that, everyone knew that Snow and Whitehead were on to something—a full 40 years before the germ theory of disease would explain how bacteria cause illness and death.

> **Through their conversations, tutors and writers connect different perspectives in a way that leads to problem solving.**

We tell this story because it seems relevant for today's high school writing centers for two reasons. First, it shows how problem solving and creative thinking occur when two people collaborate. Snow applied his medical knowledge and scientific way of thinking, and Whitehead drew upon his familiarity with the neighborhood to attack a problem for which neither man's own expertise was sufficient. Since the city council and the medical establishment could not see beyond the bad-air theory, Snow and Whitehead turned to each other.

Second, Snow and Whitehead's story shows what can be achieved by relating local and global perspectives. Snow and Whitehead's achievement was to describe the outbreak locally in a way that yielded a global view for how to stop it. Canvassing every address and recording each observation, they gathered bits of information that would eventually reveal two perspectives at once—the individual deaths in each household and the pattern of these deaths in the neighborhood. Snow's map offered a visual viewpoint from which to understand factors that could be responsible for the contagion, namely the correlation between the homes where the victims died and the pumps where they drew their water.

Just as Snow and Whitehead complemented each other, writers turn to the writing center, where the perspectives of students, instructors, and institutions intersect. Writing center tutors help students to understand these perspectives and then to negotiate them. They do so through intimate discourses that tutors and students draw upon from their experiences in the classroom and other communities to which they belong. Through their conversations, tutors and writers connect different perspectives in a way that leads to problem solving. We see this in writing centers when a student plans to write a paper one way, but their tutor reminds him or her that the assignment, and thus the reader, is asking for a different approach. We see it when tutors learn how to work with students whose language or learning style is different from their own. We also see it when directors or tutors engage faculty in conversations about ways to make their assignments clearer or more relevant to students' lives. Such conversations are difficult to achieve in a classroom where the teacher has little time for one-to-one instruction and the authority of the teacher and assignment are ever-present. They are especially difficult among colleagues who do not often share teaching ideas or, as is sometimes the case with new writing centers, misunderstand the writing center's role.

Snow and Whitehead needed both the global and the local perspectives in order to discover the source of the cholera. Today's high schools need both the global and local perspectives in order to create an accurate map of the literacy lives of all of their students. Although schools may have lists of state mandated "literacy" checks—exams, standards, benchmarks, and objectives—these only hint at the big picture, and in some ways distort it. As critics of such sweeping evaluation tools know, desperately needed information is missing, information that can only be discovered by talking to students one-to-one.

A high school writing center allows for both global and local perspectives. We see the global perspective when the writing center becomes a place that enables authentic evaluation, evaluation that reveals the stories of students' struggles and successes to an extent that other measurement tools cannot. We see the local perspective when a tutor talks with a student, getting to the heart of that individual student's questions or anxieties about and approaches to their own writing.

COLLABORATIVE LEARNING AND WRITING CENTER THEORY

The story of Snow and Whitehead is true, and we point to its value in showing the benefits of collaborative learning to illustrate concepts that comprise writing center theory. Collaborative learning lies at the core of this theory and begins with Kenneth Bruffee. In the early 1970s, he started a movement that is now reflected in thousands of writing centers worldwide. According to Bruffee (1984), the thoughts and ideas that students work with stem from the conversations they hear going on around them every day among family members, friends, teachers, and classmates and in books and media. Students internalize this talk to the point where it may become their own thoughts, and like lint in the trap of the clothes dryer, they can see their thoughts but cannot trace them back to their origin. Sharing knowledge with others, as writing requires, involves making the internalized talk social and public again; once it re-enters the public sphere, both tutor and student internalize that "talk." The cycle continues with each conversation, affecting both tutor and student, and consequently affecting teaching and learning in both classrooms and writing centers.

Bruffee's ideas are rooted in the *pragmatism* of John Dewey, emphasizing active over passive learning, and in *constructivism,* or the idea that we create meaning by joining prior knowledge with new knowledge rather than absorbing it whole. Classroom teachers know this relationship well, but so do tutors. For example, Bruffee's focus on the relationship between speech and thought, or internalized talk, reaches back to the work of Russian psychologist Lev Vygotsky and his research on *inner speech* and the *zone of proximal development.* Vygotsky's (1981) notion of language as a *mind tool* helps us see how one-to-one conversations about writing can help students improve as writers. For example, both teachers and tutors use conversation to help writers connect with what they are expected to learn or to do. They model strategies or ask questions that writers use or ask themselves as they write. That modeling helps students hear and learn a discourse, or a way to talk about writing, that they then internalize and use subsequently and eventually more efficiently as they improve as writers. That new discourse becomes a tool that students can then rely on throughout their composing process to make decisions about their own writing. The more decisions students make, the greater their agency in their own learning. Over time, this process empowers students. Not only do they begin to improve as writers, but they begin to see themselves as writers.

Also important to understanding the promise of the one-to-one conversations between tutors and students is *dialogism,* or the idea that language is relational and dynamic so that writers always write in response to something already said or written and in anticipation of responses that will follow (Bakhtin, 1981). In a writing center session, for example, we see this understanding in action when we see tutors ask writers whether they feel their draft has met the requirements of an assignment. If the writer has deviated from the expectations, the tutor might ask how the teacher might respond. Often, this is not meant to discourage the writer as much as it is to help the writer connect with the expectations of the assignment in order to make decisions about the direction of their work. Similarly, dialogism operates in the conversational interaction of a tutorial when the tutor models effective composing strategies, which then leads the writer to develop her ideas further. It also offers the tutor a way to demonstrate his or her own expertise as one who understands the writer's text as the product of a discourse they are familiar with and one they know how to anticipate a response to.

Bruffee and his contemporaries taught us that writers' words and ideas are products of social interactions and shared experiences that take place in a sea of talk. Actual conversations recede from individual memory, but they never leave entirely. They are ever-present like the musical rhythms that support a melody. When students speak or write, they do so in response not only to a teacher or an essay prompt but also to the backdrop of conversations stored in their memories; those memories help to create what the student says and support his or her ideas as they are transformed for a specific audience. "The point . . . ," Bruffee wrote, "is that writing always has its roots deep in the acquired ability to carry on the social symbolic exchange we call conversation" (1984, pp. 641–642).

The notion of conversation-infused collaborative writing centers has led some to imagine a Burkean Parlor (Lunsford, 1991/2008) in which the conversation is never-ending: Students enter the parlor, listen, contribute, and move on, only to be replaced by new students who enter, listen, contribute, and move on. The cycle continues indefinitely. Throughout it, students learn to negotiate power and control. Such negotiations can be difficult, but they are part of the responsibility of writing centers and writing center tutors' jobs. As Andrea Lunsford (1991/2008) wrote, "Such a center presents a challenge to the institution of higher education, an institution that insists on rigidly controlled individual performance, on evaluation as punishment, on isolation" (p. 52). We argue that Lunsford's assertion also works for K–12 instruction, especially given the effects of high-stakes testing on teaching and learning. In fact, both Bruffee (1994) and Lunsford (1991/2008) asserted that the instructional value of what took place within writing center conferences had the potential to change college writing instruction. That potential exists in high school writing centers as well (Childers, Fels, & Jordan, 2004; Dean, 2010; Fels, 2010; Kent, 2006).

Fostering certain kinds of conversations, like the ones that occur in a community of learners such as a writing center, can expand the range, complexity, and subtlety of tutors' and students' knowledge of the composing process and their thoughts about writing and themselves as writers. Those conversations can also help tutors and students learn how to negotiate boundaries, within which and against which each must work in the classroom and the writing center session. The theoretical concepts mentioned above are the starting point for pedagogies that empower students toward independence. In the next sections, we show you how they work.

The Unique Student–Tutor Relationship

There is a paradox in the relationship of peer tutors to teachers and the students they help. As John Trimbur (1987) pointed out, if one is qualified to tutor, they are no longer a peer. Peer tutors are tutors and peers at the same time, and they have to negotiate the tension between being a peer and being a tutor. This is a complication with which writing centers have always struggled, and peer tutors learn to manage this tension and to lean sometimes toward peer and sometimes toward tutor. But they are always students, and that part of their identity is critical to the role they play in other students' literacy lives.

For most students, high school is a time when hardly anything is more important than relationships, and hardly anyone is more influential than a trusted peer. It makes sense, then, that our pedagogies would try to take advantage of this fact to address some of the challenges that writing poses for most students, like learning to notice what is important. Because tutors are also students, they know what other students face as they try to improve as writers. They know the challenges that writers face, so they do not take for granted writers' experiences. They know that a writers' success is going to depend on their ability to connect what they know with what they are trying to learn. They listen to writers and help them sift through the confusion that naturally arises when learning something new.

Only a truly exceptional individual fights through the noise and distractions of life to stick with a problem until it becomes clear. Snow and Whitehead were two such individuals, and they helped one another to see more clearly. A teacher plays a specific role in students' learning, but students also need someone to sit with them, one-to-one, to help them notice what's important in their learning to write and in their own writing, and then to act on both. With that action comes agency, which builds over time and is essential to students' growth as writers. Students also need someone who understands their immediate or long-term feelings about an assignment or about themselves as writers. We teachers know those feelings well and work hard to encourage and motivate students. But our experience in writing centers has shown us that at the moment of need, few can do a better job of helping students through those feelings than another student.

Relationships are important to another key concept in learning to write: *noticing*. Noticing is a key concept in second language research and one developed by Richard Schmidt (1990), who realized as he was learning Portuguese that he had to notice something before he could learn it. A study by Susan Blau and John Hall (2002) showed that non-native English speaking (NNES) writers are no different than native English speaking (NES) writers when it comes to noticing features of writing that they tend to overlook. Jessica Williams's (2004) study in the *Journal of Second Language Writing* concluded that *to show* and *to explain* are effective. Instead of asking, "What is the author's perspective in the assigned text?" or telling, "This is the author's perspective," it might be better to say, "This (word or this phrase) is how you can tell the author's perspective in the assigned passage. Do you see it?"

In other words, teaching students to notice is like highlighting something that is there all along. At first glance, this would seem to be taken care of by effective classroom teaching: Tell students what to pay attention to and hold them responsible for it. But effective educators—those who are dedicated to helping students learn, not those who merely want to hold students account-able—know that teaching and learning are more complicated than this. Teach-ers can point out what students should know, but often it is someone else, perhaps a tutor, who provides the procedural knowledge of *what it feels like* to know something and to reinforce that *this is important—pay attention to it.*

> **Tutors know what other students face as they try to improve as writers because they face the same challenges. They do not take for granted what writers experience.**

A student may assume he knows how to brainstorm an idea or develop an argument, but as Harris (1995) told us, it is not until he works with a tutor that he experiences *how it feels* to turn off his internal editor and let ideas flow without discarding them right off the bat. Similarly, a writer may know what he ought to do, but only his tutor can provide the motivation he needs to stay engaged to completion (Childers, Fels, & Jordan, 2004; Fallon, 2010).

The kind of learning that occurs with tutors is made possible in part because it does not occur in a classroom, where students might see only the authority of the teacher and the expectations of the assignment. In the classroom, students may be shy and afraid to speak up when they don't understand. Rather than embarrass themselves, they remain silent. Or, they do just the opposite and act as if they understand when they do not. All of these tensions are directly tied to students' agency for their own learning. It may seem strange to think of students as agents of their own learning. After all, teachers are often held responsible for what students learn or do not learn. But when we grant students agency in what they learn, we help them act upon it. They notice, and they internalize what they learn. They then own it. Without agency, students remain disengaged, unable to act upon what they need to learn. Over time, disengagement and the feelings associated with it become part of students' identities. Learning in a writing center or elsewhere depends on a writer's willingness to admit what they don't know, to take risks, and to open themselves up to possibilities. For most students, this kind of learning is about feeling connected. In a writing center, tutors can better help students engage because they understand students' struggles. Tutors also understand that their job is one of helping. Thus, the relationship between tutor and student is important to students' potential ability to notice what they need to do in order to improve as a writer. For that to happen, the writer must trust that the tutor cares enough about them to keep them from falling flat on their faces. Let's now take a look at what else the relationship between tutor and writer makes possible.

Demystifying Academic Discourse

Students' ability to use and understand academic discourse is crucial to their success in high school and college, and writing center tutors' guidance can be an invaluable resource. The amount, content, and style of reading material can sometimes pose obstacles to students. The language of teachers' assignments can also be difficult to understand. What might seem obvious to teachers is often not so obvious to students. For example, we have all had students whose diverse backgrounds lead to confusion when assignments expect them to draw upon cultural knowledge they do not have. This is especially true for immigrant students who are expected to understand the significance of iconic historical moments like civil rights protests or the settling of the prairie. At times like these, tutors not only demonstrate their skills as readers and writers, but they also call upon their own knowledge backgrounds and experience with teachers' assignments to help demystify reading and writing assignments for students. For some students, school can become their Mount Everest—a long, hard, solitary slog. It is worth pointing out that professional mountain climbers never attempt to scale Everest without the aid of sherpas who help them navigate the route, translate messages, resupply teams, and prepare mentally. Tutors are like sherpas because they draw upon their own experiences to assist students in reading or interpreting the signals in an assignment, supplying ideas, and negotiating the academic boundaries imposed on them.

> **Whereas teachers have many students and little time to get to know individuals, tutors can help each student gain proficiency in language and literacy.**

Consider the potential of one-to-one tutoring to help students with limited English proficiency enter high school. By 2008, according to the National Clearinghouse for English Language Acquisition (NCELA), nearly 5.5 million English Language Learners (ELLs), those students who speak a language other than English in the home, attended America's public schools (NCELA, para. 1, n.d.). By 2010, more than one in six people 5 years of age or older spoke a language in the home other than English (U.S. Census Bureau, Language Use section, 2010). ELL students are a significant part of schools' student populations. By the time these students reach high school and college, they are referred to by many labels—residents, immigrants, language minority students, bilinguals or multilinguals, Generation 1.5, and so on—that hint at their diverse and complex identities. Adding to that complexity is that there is no uniformity among different states' notions of English proficiency. When students move from one state to another, they risk being placed in classrooms where there is little support for their language learning needs because they are presumed to be more proficient than they truly are. Whereas teachers have many students and little time to get to know each one, tutors can help individual students gain proficiency in language and literacy. Tutors might also discover that a student who speaks English with an accent can write in English as well as any of his native English-speaking peers. These discoveries require the attention of and are made possible by the kind of one-to-one relationship that only tutors and students can have.

Authority and Agency

Writing centers can also help to shift students toward greater independent learning. Composition traditionalists might say that students need drill and practice, but as Muriel Harris (1995) pointed out in a lucid article on the benefits of peer tutoring, research indicates the opposite. In fact, students want their independence and freedom of choice, and what they say about their tutors' ability to help them achieve this is revealing. Among the student comments Harris pointed to are:

"I like how she wanted answers from me. She didn't just tell me how to write."

"He helps you understand more what you're doing by having you do it yourself."

"She knows how to help without giving answers. She makes me think." (p. 30)

Harris explained,

Even non-directive, student-centered teachers who see their advice and suggestions as open-ended possibilities their students can freely reject should recognize that such suggestions are often not taken precisely as they are intended. Students feel freer to develop their own ideas in settings other than teacher/student conversations. (p. 31)

Students often feel freer to develop their own ideas when talking with a tutor than when talking with their teacher because of the peer factor. This is something Bruffee recognized early on when developing his ideas about the value of collaborative learning. Students' community of peers, including their tutors, creates the conversation or discourse that students internalize, make their own, and are then enfranchised to speak on their own. Throughout this process, tutors and writers create knowledge for themselves and others. Bruffee (1984) advised:

> Our task must involve engaging students in conversations among themselves at as many points in both the writing and the reading process as possible, and . . . we should contrive to ensure that students' conversation about what they read and write is similar in as many ways as possible to the way we would like them eventually to read and write. (p. 642)

Teachers and the authority they represent are part of the reason why tutors can be effective. A tutoring session actually magnifies what the teacher says in the classroom. As you listen to a tutoring session, you can hear how students dissect, apply, and reflect upon the voices of teachers echoing in their heads: "He said we need to . . . ," "I don't get why she wants us to . . . ," "Can I do . . . ?" This is learning at its best, with teachers pushing students into a new and unfamiliar discourse, students wrestling with it, and tutors nudging them toward claiming authority over it.

FINAL THOUGHTS

Let's return now to Dr. Snow and the Reverend Whitehead back in London in 1854. Nearly everyone at the time assumed that cholera came from bad-smelling air. There was certainly enough of it in London at the time. But Snow and Whitehead could not rest until they knew for certain, and so they gathered data from each house and apartment in the locality and assembled as much information as they could, taking careful notes as Snow created a map that revealed the big picture of where the victims had died. The two men persisted despite little hope of success, enduring ridicule because they opened their minds to a new way of seeing. In the end, Snow and Whitehead set in motion the unique power of the one-to-one for making a large-scale difference in people's lives.

Just as Snow and Whitehead needed both the global and the local perspectives in order to discover the source of London's cholera outbreak, today's high schools need both global and local perspectives on their students' literacy lives. State-mandated tests and standards are no substitute for talking to students one-to-one and uncovering their fears, hopes, and true potential. By showing students how to negotiate discourses from their homes, communities, and classrooms, writing center tutors help students adopt new perspectives and then apply their thoughts to writing. Through collaborative conversations, tutors help students notice what has been there all along, whether that is internal, like the student's own knowledge or skills, or external, like the academic discourse that can appear in a text or an assignment. When students notice, they gain agency over their learning, learning that may have otherwise felt undecipherable or out of reach. The high school writing center is a place where the needs of students, teachers, and schools intersect, and through the power of the one-to-one, those needs can be met in ways unimagined.

REFERENCES

Bakhtin, M. M. (1981). *The dialogic imagination: Four essays* (M. Holquist, Ed., C. Emerson & M. Holquist, Trans.). Austin: University of Texas Press.

Blau, S., & Hall, J. (2002). Guilt-free tutoring: Rethinking how we tutor non-native English speaking students. *The Writing Center Journal 23*(1), 23–44.

Bruffee, K. (1984). Collaborative learning and the conversation of mankind. *College English 46*(7), 635–652.

Bruffee, K. (1994). Making the most of knowledgeable peers. *Change 26*(3), 39.

Childers, P. B., Fels, D., & Jordan, J. (2004, Fall). The secondary school writing center: A place to build confident, competent writers. *Praxis: A Writing Center Journal 2*(1). Retrieved from http://projects.uwc.utexas.edu/praxis/?q=node/91

Dean, C. (2010). The ecology of peer tutoring: Perspectives of student staff in one high school writing center. (Doctoral dissertation). Retrieved from ProQuest. (AAT 3415470)

Fallon, B. (2010). *The perceived, conceived, and lived experiences of 21st century peer writing tutors* (Unpublished doctoral dissertation). Indiana University of Pennsylvania, Indiana, Pennsylvania.

Fels, D. (2010). The vernacular architecture of composition instruction: What the voices of writing center tutors reveal about standardized instruction and assessment. (Doctoral dissertation). Retrieved from ProQuest. (AAT 3413161)

Harris, M. (1995). Talking in the middle: Why writers need writing tutors. *College English 57*(1), 27–42.

Johnson, S. (2006). *The ghost map.* New York: Riverhead/Penguin.

Kent, R. (2006). *A guide to creating student-staffed writing centers, grades 6–12.* New York: Peter Lang.

Lunsford, A. (1991/2008). Collaboration, control, and the idea of a writing center. In C. Murphy & S. Sherwood (Eds.), *The St. Martin's sourcebook for writing center tutors* (3rd ed., pp. 47–52). Boston: Bedford/St. Martin's.

National Clearinghouse for English Language Acquisition. (n.d.). *Frequently asked questions.* Retrieved from http://www.ncela.gwu.edu/faqs/

Schmidt, R. (1990). The role of consciousness in second language learning. *Applied Linguistics 11*, 129–158.

Trimbur, J. (1987). Peer tutoring: A contradiction in terms? *The Writing Center Journal* 7(2), 21–28.

U.S. Census Bureau. (2010). Detailed language spoken at home and ability to speak English for the population 5 years and older by states: 2006–2008 (ACS) [Data file]. Retrieved from http://www.census.gov/hhes/socdemo/language/index.html

Vygotsky, L. S. (1981). The genesis of higher mental functions. In J. Wertsch (Ed.), *The concept of activity in Soviet psychology* (pp. 144–188). White Plains, NY: M. Sharpe.

Williams, J. (2004). Tutoring and revision: Second language writers in the writing center. *Journal of Second Language Writing 13*, 173–201.

CHAPTER TWO

Change I Can See

A High School English Teacher's Perspective of the Writing Center's Impact on Bilingual, Hispanic Students

Katherine Palacio and Kevin Dvorak

Freshmen sit nervously in their seats as they wait for their very first writing assignment of their high school career. I explain that they will be completing a writing sample so that I can assess their different skill levels, and worried eyes look back at me. After I distribute the handouts, which have a creative, yet simple prompt, a few students anxiously bring pen to paper, while the majority sit and stare at the blank lines in front of them. I offer a few words of encouragement, followed by a gentle reminder that this is not a graded assignment, and the students' expressions change to one of confusion. I soon realize that these students are mainly concerned with the capital letter that is usually given on the top margin of each completed assignment. As the clock ticks, I feel their frustrations intensify, and another student has stopped trying. I think, *This has to change.*

THE CHALLENGES OF TEACHING WRITING

Monsignor Edward Pace High School (Pace, for short), is located in Miami, Florida, in a county where two-thirds of the households speak Spanish as the primary language at home (U.S. Census Bureau, 2008). Seventy percent of Pace's student population is Hispanic, and so when our students leave school, many return to homes where Spanish is the primary—or only—language of communication. For many Hispanic students, "literacy in English develops in school settings and is not reinforced in homes where grandparents, parents, other relatives, and family friends speak some version of . . . Spanish; where books, newspapers, and other reading materials are rare; and where family comes above everything else" (Mendez Newman, 2003, p. 47). Our students' school experiences with English haven't been uniformly positive. Many have shared that they feel they aren't good at writing because they have grammar and spelling mistakes, or they had received low grades in their middle school grammar classes. To most of our students, writing equals grammar, and grammar equals bad grades.

So, as an English teacher, I wanted to prove to students that writing wasn't just about grammar and grades, but how? In a room full of nearly 30 students, all with different writing skill levels, I wondered about the best way to help them develop as writers. I believe that each student has his or her own level of "personal best," so how could I grade 30 papers, keeping each individual student's ability in mind, and return them in a timely fashion? How do teachers do that with 5 or 6 classes of 30 students each? I wanted to find a way to be able to teach and reach every student in my classroom, and given the number of students in each class, that was not going to be an easy task.

> **To most of our students, writing equals grammar, and grammar equals bad grades.**

SHARING A FENCE AND BRIDGING THE GAP

Pace shares a fence with St. Thomas University (STU), where, in the summer of 2009, I was taking a graduate course in grammar and composition. The professor, Dr. Kevin Dvorak, was also the director of the University Writing Center (UWC); I was unfamiliar with writing centers at the time, but as I listened to him discuss the services that the UWC provided for the university, I realized that this was the type of learning environment I was interested in bringing to the high school.

Reflecting on the frustrations of my own students, I asked for his opinion on what I could do. I was thrilled to find out that his senior tutor, Denise, had recently completed a research study on ways to bridge the gap between high school writing and college writing. As a result, she was looking for a high school to work with, one that would allow the UWC tutors to work with high school students. Kevin and I thought this would be an excellent opportunity for both schools. Not only would his tutors gain experience working with high school students, but my own students would have additional, outside help after school in my own classroom, free of charge. Since many of St. Thomas's students share the same language and/or cultural background as Pace's students, we knew the tutors would likely be able to relate to our students, but we also knew we would have to create an atmosphere where students could feel comfortable and not intimidated by the tutors. Both Kevin and I wanted this partnership to be successful.

Logistics of Our High School/College Collaboration

Once both institutions approved of our plan, we spent the summer making sure that all persons involved would be prepared to follow proper protocol for working in a Catholic high school. Since St. Thomas University is also a Catholic institution, Kevin and his staff were familiar with the process. The tutors were required by the Archdiocese to complete a child-abuse awareness training session, Virtus, and to go through a fingerprint background check. While I moved furniture to a classroom that was larger, newer, and could serve as the writing center after school, Kevin created a schedule around his tutors' college courses or writing center hours. It worked out that the tutors would be able to work with us twice a week after school for one hour and spend Friday mornings with teachers and students during class time.

During our first English department meeting of the school year, I gave my colleagues the great news: Pace was going to have its own writing center with college tutors twice a week after school for free! And as an added bonus, the college tutors would be on campus every Friday during the school day to assist teachers and students. Everyone seemed excited. Just the thought of having extra assistance during research paper time was enough to keep them smiling. But we already had a very busy schedule. I knew that not every teacher could easily find the time to implement the writing center's services into their schedules.

Not Just Another Fad Program

We teachers are often presented with new programs or ideas that are supposed to change everything for the better. After a while, it can be hard to take any of these programs seriously; we've grown used to programs being replaced by the next new thing the following year. So, while Denise had already conducted her own study on high school- and college-level writing, I needed to do some research of my own to assure my colleagues and administration that this wasn't just another fad program. I read all the books and journal articles on writing center research and theory I could get my hands on, and I relied on Kevin's expertise in the field. As a result, in any flyer, brochure, or email that was written to publicize our new writing center, I made sure to include that this was a research-based project and not just an experiment. I shared with my colleagues that "Writing centers create an environment where writers can bounce their ideas off others, questions can lead to new ideas, writing for self or publication can blossom, and resources on writing abound" (Childers, Fels, & Jordan, 2004, para. 8). My hope was that faculty would see that our writing center could really make a difference in how our students were learning to write, so that students wouldn't doubt their abilities or have fear in their eyes when teachers assigned a paper.

The First Class Visit

I was really looking forward to the first Friday that the tutors would be in my classroom helping my students, but I was also nervous. On one hand, I knew that having tutors in my classroom during school hours meant that each of us would be able to focus on one small group of students at a time. On the other hand, I knew my students still thought writing class meant they would do a lot of work and still get an F at the end because their writing just wasn't "good enough."

I prepared the students for the tutors' visit by sharing that we would have "helpers," college students who were very good writers and wanted to help them improve their writing. The students still seemed apprehensive, so I explained that the tutors weren't teachers who were grading the work; they were going to be motivators and supporters of their work.

On Friday, the tutors arrived before class so I could discuss the assignment the students were working on with them. My students are typically very talkative as they walk through the door, giving each other the latest version of "high-fives" and talking about their previous class. But that Friday was different. As my students shuffled into the room, they became very quiet when they saw the two strangers. At first, as the tutors began to try to work with small groups of students, the students responded with silence and resistance. But then the tutors decided to change tactics. They shared some of their own writing experiences and setbacks. This made the students feel at ease with

> I needed to do some research of my own to assure my colleagues and administration that this wasn't just another fad program.

them. The tutors asked the students about their own backgrounds and what the students liked to do after school. Their attempts to find common ground worked. The students responded by opening up. Intrigued by the fact that the tutors were young but also ambitious, the students asked the tutors questions. They were impressed by the tutors' double majors and minors, such as Denise's majors in religious studies and professional writing. The students seemed more comfortable after those initial, casual conversations.

The tutors then turned their attention back to the students in the small groups, and something amazing happened. The students started to take on leadership roles and helped group members who struggled with the writing prompt. Others would offer their opinions of the writing that was being read aloud, and they would raise their hands and ask the tutors—not me—for help. I loved it. These students were comfortable with the tutors, and they didn't want me to check their work until the tutors approved of it. These students were learning the benefits of peer editing, peer revision, and peer tutoring, all in just one class.

When it came time to collect their assignments, I saw dramatic improvements in the quality of my students' work. There were minimal grammatical errors, and most students added the details I was looking for. As a result, they wrote more. If this was what every Friday was going to be like, I was in for a treat, and so were my colleagues.

In-Class Tutors Help Students Hear Teacher Feedback

When I saw how much my students and I were benefiting from the Friday sessions, I couldn't contain my enthusiasm when I talked with my department colleagues. As research paper time approached, Carmen, the junior literature teacher, approached me about requesting the tutors for a Friday session, and I scheduled a workshop with the tutors and her students. At this point, a third tutor had joined the group, and I let the tutors know that the students were writing a paper on Arthur Miller's *The Crucible*. Carmen was frustrated because the students didn't seem to be making improvements based on her suggestions.

> **The students had already listened to these suggestions before, but the tutors helped them really *hear* them.**

When the tutors arrived at the junior literature classroom, Carmen separated the class into three groups, depending on the students' chosen essay topic. Each tutor joined a group, and as soon as the tutor was done giving his or her suggestions, based on what Carmen had already explained, the students would work intently on revising their essay. Each would take turns reading their revisions out loud. Then the tutor would suggest that they work with a partner on revising a second or third time. Meanwhile, Carmen expressed to me that she finally noticed that the students understood what she had been trying to explain to them. "Sometimes it takes someone else to explain it, and it just clicks," she expressed to me. "I've tried to explain it a few different ways, but it's hard to reach out to the kids this way with only one teacher and so many students." The students had already listened to these suggestions before, but the tutors helped them really *hear* them.

Afterschool Tutors Help Students Develop Confidence

Although the demand for Friday in-class sessions soared, the afterschool sessions were slow to take off. However, once two freshman literature teachers decided to make the afterschool visits a part of their class requirements, the pace picked up. They assigned groups of six to eight students to visit the writing center, and I emailed the teachers to let them know when the students attended a session.

Some of these were my own writing students, so they were already familiar with the tutors. They knew the tutors by name, and some even had preferences as to which tutor they wanted to work with. For these students, coming to the writing center started off as a requirement, but each session became a learning experience. The writing center was not an "all work and no play" space; it was a space where people of similar backgrounds and future expectations could work together. Tutors and students shared stories, they laughed, and they got down to business when it was time.

These students weren't required to stay the entire hour, but most of them wanted to. There are many reasons why students were staying past the hour in the writing center: Some had practice off-campus after school, some had to stay at a friend's house until their parents finished work, and some had other homework assignments to complete at home. Many of the students we saw in the writing center had to complete the essays before heading home, where their parents were not sure how to help them. Either their parents spoke a different language or did not have a strong enough grasp of the English language to feel like they could help. Since the tutors helped the students feel more confident about themselves as writers, these students understood how to take what they'd learned in the writing center and continue working on their writing *at home*.

The Writers' Studio Reaches Out to Parents

Since we knew that, for many of our students' parents, speaking and understanding very little English was a problem when it came to helping their kids at home with schoolwork, we knew we needed to reach out to the parents. Though we have resources on the Web that parents can check, such as class pages for every teacher that include homework assignments, news, and grades, not all parents are comfortable with the technology, especially those who have difficulty reading in English. Additionally, many of our families don't have access to computers or the Internet at home. Students knew they could come to the center for help with their writing assignments, but were parents getting that message?

So I decided to use the traditional "letter to parents." I typed up a letter that let parents know that we have a writing center with skilled college tutors from St. Thomas University. My students brought back the letter, signed by their parents, and I thought, *Hopefully, that will help spread the word.* And it did. I received emails from two parents, explaining that their children needed extra help at school. Because the parents were not comfortable speaking English at home, they were not proficient in writing in English, and they wanted the tutors to help their children. I replied to the email with additional information about our center, such as the hours, the background of the tutors, and the fact that tutoring was free, and I let them know that I would notify them when their children did attend the sessions, so they could keep track of how many visits the students made.

> **Parents stayed behind to ask more questions about it. They had never heard of a writing center, and they were looking for a school that could help their students' progress.**

Our vice principal had also received an email from a parent who asked about tutoring services on campus. This parent also needed a writing tutor for her children because she wasn't sure how to help them with writing assignments. The VP told the parent a bit about our writing center and gave the parent my contact information.

During Open House, an annual event where parents of prospective students are invited to our campus for informational sessions and tours, our English department chair spoke a bit about the writing center, and two parents stayed behind to ask more questions about it. They had never heard of a writing center, and they were looking for a school that could help their students' progress academically. I took the opportunity to give them as many details as I could in the short time I had, and they seemed impressed. Private schools tend to compete with one another to attract students, and having a writing center became not only an asset for teachers and students but for our overall marketing campaign as well.

REFLECTIONS ON THE FIRST YEAR

Throughout the first year, I was constantly taking note of what worked, what didn't work, and what needed improvement. Unfortunately, somewhere along the way, the writing center became associated only with the English department, and no matter how many reminders I sent out, the English teachers were the main ones sending students with research papers and essays. While groups of students have come from AP History classes to get feedback on their document-based question essays, and while the math department added one research writing assignment to its curriculum, I sometimes wondered if, by requesting other departments to bring their students to the writing center, they might feel as though I was checking to see if they were including writing in their curriculum. From my colleagues who work in high school writing centers across the country, I have heard that this is common: Sometimes other teachers think that the writing center is trying to take over or police their jobs. I also know that building relationships and establishing trust takes time, so I hope that with continued outreach and effort, more faculty will realize how the writing center can help them in their classrooms.

In the summer between the first and second year, Kevin and I met to brainstorm ways to continue building on the momentum of what was working, while addressing what I thought wasn't working. Aside from finding new ways to get the word out, I wanted the room to stand apart from any other room on campus. By the time the center opened for its second year in September, the writing center had a new name, a new look, a new website, and a new crop of tutors. The Writers' Studio now had large black tables in place of student desks and 10 brand-new computers. I created a website with facts about the center and bios of the tutors. I also updated the informational brochure with pictures of the students working in the center. Kevin started a peer tutoring program where Pace's top students would attend professional tutoring workshops in the UWC and help in our writing center. The writing center now had many aliases: a workspace, an idea starter, a safe space, the list goes on. At Pace, we try to make the center beneficial to all the stakeholders: parents, teachers, and students. Without any one of these parts, the center would not be successful.

FINAL THOUGHTS

The world of writing center research was new to me, and I'm glad it's something I became involved in. When I began looking at the literature on secondary writing centers, I found information on how to create and manage writing centers, but only a few articles addressed the issue of confidence levels in high school students. Based on what I observed happening in our own center, the most striking change in the students was the increase in their confidence as writers. Self-efficacy research has shown that when a student feels like they have the resources they need and can achieve an outcome they want, they are more likely to be motivated, to try new approaches, and to persevere (Pajares, 2003). This is absolutely what I witnessed, and so, when we think about increasing the writing skills of our students, especially those with low confidence like many of our Hispanic students, programs that help increase confidence with writing will also help students increase their skill with writing. A writing center program does both.

One year later, a new group of freshmen sits nervously in their seats as they wait for their very first writing assignment of their high school career. The similarities to the previous year are striking: They are slow to start and quick to finish, and the frustration in the air is achingly familiar. After we spend about 20 minutes discussing their responses, the conversation leads into how they feel about writing, and again, they complain about grammar and receiving poor grades in the past. However, this year, I have something new, a way to offer them hope that I didn't have before. I take the opportunity to explain the writing centers' services, and I distribute the letter with information to each student. When they hear that the college students will be volunteering their time to support them, to partner with them and help them develop more confidence in their writing, their worried faces soften. In that moment, they begin to walk away from the path of resistance and toward the path of growth: They are ready to continue on their writing adventure. I think, *This is the change I hoped to see.*

REFERENCES

Childers, P. B., Fels, D., & Jordan, J. (2004). The secondary school writing center: A place to build confident, competent writers. *Praxis: A Writing Center Journal, 2*(1). Retrieved from http://projects.uwc.utexas.edu/praxis/?q=node/91

Mendez Newman, B. (2003). Centering in the borderlands: The writing center at Hispanic-serving institutions. *The Writing Center Journal, 23*(2), 45–64.

Miller, A. (1953). *The Crucible.* New York: Viking Press.

Pajares, F. (2003). Self-efficacy beliefs, motivation, and achievement in writing: A review of the literature. *Reading and Writing Quarterly, 19,* 139–158.

U.S. Census Bureau. (2008). *Miami-Dade County, Florida.* Retrieved from http://pewhispanic.org/states/?countyid=12086

CHAPTER THREE

The Idea of a High School Writing Center

Kerri Mulqueen

This chapter traces the learning curve my colleagues and I experienced as we developed our writing center at Nazareth Regional High School, a 450-student parochial high school in the Brooklyn neighborhood of East Flatbush. Our school serves an area where the population is nearly 95% African-American and Latino-American, with a predominance of West Indian roots. More than half of Nazareth's students receive some form of need-based financial aid. In 2007, an informal student survey conducted by the school showed that two-thirds of the students live in single-parent homes, and more than one-third of students live with caregivers whose first language is not English. Because many of Nazareth's students speak another language at home and come through local elementary schools that do not necessarily provide adequate resources, personalized support is imperative to their academic growth and success.

Our writing center provides that support for those and other students by offering help with written assignments or navigating academic language. In this chapter, I describe our approach to getting faculty to buy into a new center, as well as our approach to recruiting and training an eclectic group of peer tutors. By including reflections from the tutors themselves, I share how student leaders became tutors and how tutors became student leaders. I then return to the writing center theorists whose work guided my ideas about creating the center and reflect on those theories in light of the realities involved in sustaining a high school writing center. I conclude by considering the potential for high school writing centers to transform the literacy lives of students not just at our high school but all high schools.

What I learned as a tutor in the SUNY Albany Writing Center with Steve North foregrounds my work as a high school teacher. I learned that a tutor's priority was to help writers develop as writers, and the best thing I could do was to help the writer think about their writing in a different way. I found that writers need to talk about writing in order to get better at it, and I learned to listen closely to students and to individualize instruction and response. Whether I worked one-on-one with Brazilian-born Ph.D. candidates or locally born commuter freshmen—all of whom struggled to make the transition to college expectations—I encouraged students to talk to me about their work, their goals, and their struggles to get ideas down on paper. Doing so gave voice to their concerns, which began the process of getting past them. Seeing their writing in a different way helped students engage with good writing habits and embrace revision as less of a devil than they thought it was. After working with these students for some time, I noticed how little cracks would begin to open in the walls students formed between themselves and their work, revealing paths toward progress more clearly. Because writing can be such an isolating process, those discoveries were tremendously heartening for students.

I carried the writing conference method into my high school classroom and was able to avoid the disillusionment that so often hits young teachers as they realize they cannot reach all students with the same methods. I came to judge my work according to perceptible changes in the writer's thinking or behavior rather than the paper's quality or polish. I touched base with each student as they worked to complete long-term projects. I wanted to hear them tell me (and tell themselves) what stymied them and what they envisioned their end result to be. Using a multi-draft process, I learned to look for students' progress. I understood that final drafts that at first glance appeared unsuccessful might actually be testament to monumental progress, so I built into each grading rubric a score for improvement.

Though I successfully put what I learned as a writing center tutor to work in my high school English class, it wasn't until I returned to graduate school and sat within earshot of tutoring sessions at the St. John's University writing center that I realized that no teacher could engage with each of their 30 students per period as deeply as peer tutors engage with writers in one-on-one sessions. Soon after, my personal mission to bring writing center work to Nazareth Regional High School began.

BRINGING A WRITING CENTER TO LIFE

With Laurel Black's (1998) concept of using writing conferences to "reduce tension in the classroom" (p. 4), I walked into the principal's office at Nazareth Regional High School just before winter break to pitch my former boss the idea of launching a writing center on the premises. Once I established that I would make myself available as point person, planner, and director, and that there would be no immediate financial cost to the school, my journey as a writing center director was under way.

In the weeks that followed, I spoke with colleagues about the potential benefits of a writing center and peer tutoring program for our school. I discussed the most crucial characteristics to look for in prospective tutors with guidance counselors and teachers. I stressed to them that it was most important that they identify excellent communicators rather than just excellent writers. I explained that much of the effectiveness of writing center conferences comes from tutor-to-student rapport, and interpersonal connections can effect change in students' composing habits. I talked specifically with English and social studies content-area teachers about the ways in which I saw writing center work deepening their students' connection with course material and understanding of assignments. With the idea in mind that "literacy is not culturally neutral" (Grimm, 1999, p. 45), I imagined a space where student-to-student conversations about schoolwork could bridge some of the cultural and generational divides that often keep teachers and students from fully understanding one another. For the struggling or disconnected student, in particular, peer tutors could act as tour guides.

> **Much of the effectiveness of writing center conferences comes from tutor and student rapport, and interpersonal communications can effect change in students' composing habits.**

As the high school personnel worked to identify possible tutors for our pilot program, I worked with the directors of the St. John's writing center to design a training workshop wherein college tutors could mentor the high school tutor trainees. The following February, a dozen Nazareth juniors came to the Institute for Writing Studies at St. John's for a half-day training session. We held a roundtable discussion about writing. The high school tutors observed the college tutors at work, and the college tutors held conferences with the high school tutors, who brought work with them in order to get a feel for being on the receiving end of a session. We followed up our half-day session at St. John's with a half-day session 2 weeks later at Nazareth, feeling it was important to empower Nazareth's tutors on their home turf and to show that writing center ideas and practices can work in any space. During our second meeting, the high schoolers tutored the college students, and we also engaged in role-playing exercises where college tutors played the part of reluctant or defensive writers, allowing the high school tutors to brainstorm ways of moving sessions forward by bringing writers more directly into the conversation.

In all of our sessions, we focused on Steve North's (1984) idea that "a tutor's job has most to do with the writer, not the text, and the direction of any tutorial derives from the writer" (p. 436). Feedback from all concerned in the weeks that followed was exceedingly positive, with Cherylin, a tutor-trainee, noting that her big takeaway from the experience was that "giving your client confidence is key." And my strategy of involving non-honors students in the tutoring program was affirmed by another trainee, Coya, who told me, "At first I was a little skeptical about joining because I didn't think that I could be capable to help another student with their English when I am not the best at mine, but the tutors at St. John's helped me realize that you're not there to fix it for them but to help them fix it themselves. "Through their training, the students began to see how they could be transformed into tutors.

Choosing Eclectic Tutors for a Diverse Center

Recruiting good communicators rather than only honor students paid off. Diversity among tutors' grade point averages, academic success, experiences, and social standing helped break down the possible hierarchy that comes with a "good student helping poor student" approach, which often leaves the struggling learners diffident and defensive. By the sheer force of their personalities and positions in the school, this eclectic mix of students helped make our writing center a space of both diversity and welcome.

Once I knew more about their personalities, I was able to match tutors with specific types of students. I learned which tutor would have the most success with the cool kids who did not respond well to being sent for extra help, and I learned which of my tutors was the best fit for helping to edit creative writing projects with Nazareth's budding artists. One tutor, Ifeomo—who had several younger siblings and volunteered as a Sunday school teacher—was best at communicating with the nervous ninth-graders on their level. Another, Marshall—who was destined to go on to an Ivy League career himself—was the junior confident enough to sit down with seniors and work on college application essays and research papers.

Peer Tutors for Every Kind of Student

It is a misconception that there are types of students who need so much help that they cannot be served by peer tutors in a high school writing center. More important than my ability to match tutors to students was the tutors' ability to adapt what they had learned from their initial training to work with anyone who walked through the door. For example, a junior student with a known individualized educational plan (IEP) for learning disabilities that included processing delays came into the center in our early weeks of operation looking for help with his science homework. His task was to read and summarize articles from the Tuesday "Science Times" section of *The New*

York Times and then write a paragraph making connections between what he had read and what he was learning in his class. When Sheila, one of our tutors, began peppering him with questions, the student quickly became overwhelmed and intimidated. He visibly withdrew and offered only monosyllabic responses. I called Sheila over, reminded her that the student had come of his own accord, and that he was already confused enough in class; our job was to lessen that feeling, not add to it. I asked her to take it one question at a time and to work with him on locating concrete answers to each of the questions she posed before jumping to another topic. She returned to her session with him, and I saw her make the necessary adjustments. As a result, the student left our center that afternoon, confident about the homework he completed. He returned a half dozen times before the end of the school year, always requesting to work with Sheila, who succeeded in making him feel both confident and capable of achieving. Sheila made discoveries of her own, reporting to me in post-session feedback, "I never realized how differently from me some people learn and think." Sheila's comments were echoed by her colleague Carla, who reported to me in emailed feedback, "People work at different paces. If you are tutoring someone and they are taking a while to understand what is being said, it is good to just break everything apart piece by piece and help the person understand what you are trying to show them." Sheila's experience and Carla's thoughtful feedback are examples of how the individual strengths of the 12 tutors began to surface almost immediately to benefit the students with whom they worked.

One of our early "regulars" in the writing center was a sophomore student who immigrated to Brooklyn from Haiti during the summer between his freshman and sophomore years in high school. When he enrolled at Nazareth, he spoke almost no English, save what little he had picked up from popular music and syndicated television. Because we have a large Haitian population at our school, we were able to pair him up with a Creole-speaking junior who translated the homework assignments and class notes and helped him communicate with his teachers before and after school. But, as you might expect, he needed more assistance than what was available in those isolated encounters. On the recommendation of his English teacher and because he recognized me from summer school, he started coming to the writing center during our after school hours, bringing written-down English assignments that he didn't know how to begin. I paired him with one of our most self-assured tutors, Tishawna, guessing that she would be the least flustered by the language barrier. My guess turned out to be correct because what my tutor was able to offer him was a patient, clear, and concise explanation of what was expected. From an unobtrusive distance, I observed their sessions. I heard the student's halting questions as he tried out new terms he heard in class: rubric, Regents, rhetoric. I also heard Tishawna's answers, coming at the student's queries from different angles, again and again, until she found an explanation that made sense to him and helped him to write.

Tishawna's determined approach to tutoring and her refusal to take "no" for an answer in the writing center mirrored her behavior on the softball field where she was also a team captain, pushing younger teammates to progress toward better play. This approach worked in both arenas but never more clearly than when she firmly nudged her weekly tutee to read his fledgling paragraphs aloud, even when he protested. Although the student's voice was quiet, and he looked at her frequently for confirmation of his pronunciation, it didn't take a trained eye to see that his and Tishawna's interactions helped his facility with language. The help the student received in the center went beyond just what ended up on the page of looseleaf handed in for class.

Student Leaders Becoming Peer Tutors

A high school writing center enables tutors who are leaders in other, possibly nonacademic areas of the school to become academic leaders as well. As a result, students who look up to those leaders may be more academically motivated when they see their club president or team captain tutoring in the writing center. For example, Yafeu, the point guard of our varsity basketball team, was a tutor. His presence suddenly made our center a more palatable place for struggling athletes to visit when they were sweating their grades and worried about eligibility for spring sports. A student in my English class was struggling to keep his grade up throughout the fall, and I wasn't having any success motivating him through one-on-one conversations, student-selected projects, or conversations with his parents. The student's offhand comment in class one day clued me in to the fact that he was currently restricted from playing on the varsity basketball team. Knowing the influence that our head coach generally exerts over his players, I stopped in the basketball office and told the coach about the difficulties his player was having; I also reminded him about the writing center and our hours of operation. He listened and said he would make sure to have a talk with my student. On our next tutoring day, my student walked into the writing center and was a little startled to recognize a teammate among our staff. I paired him up with Yafeu, the point guard, and their sessions were productive from the start because there was a built-in mentor/mentee relationship already present from the dynamic of their relationship as starter/sub on the basketball team. Because the junior student wanted to stay eligible to play, and because he did not have any issue taking directions from Yafeu, he worked toward a better understanding of the English assignments. Consequently, better effort and better grades followed.

Peer Tutors Become Student Leaders

A high school writing center can also make student leaders out of peer tutors; it can be a place for those who didn't realize their leadership potential to discover it. Kabira, one of my tutors and a member of the girls' step and cheerleading squads, had been cited at the beginning of her senior year by multiple staff members for her displays of attitude and lack of cooperation. However, she turned out to be a terrific tutor, quick to crack jokes and break down walls between "us" and "them" in sessions. Our assistant principal made a point at year's end to tell me how far they thought Kabira had come and that they saw the leadership she had developed in the writing center feeding into her demeanor and in other school activities and settings.

Around this time I also received an email out of the blue from Mrs. Roberts, one of our guidance counselors. She wanted to let me know that Ifeomo had taken it upon himself to organize study groups for foreign language and physics students as they approached final exams. She said he was not only rounding up the students for the groups but also organizing meeting places and times and admonishing anyone who signed up but did not attend. She said that she had never before seen one student take such an administrative position in an effort to help not just his own academic prospects but those of his peers. She said she figured his work in the center had something to do with these extracurricular efforts.

Zuma, one of my tutors, had taken it upon herself to drop into a ninth-grade English classroom on her free periods to check on the progress of one of her regular tutees, a reluctant writer with whom she had formed a big sister–type bond. Not only was the teacher impressed with Zuma's commitment to seeing the student succeed, but she also saw a similar commitment reflected in the freshman student, who now had another person who was looking out for them and whom she did not want to disappoint.

Tutors Embody the Mission of the Writing Center

A writing center exists not in its physical location but in the tutors who embody the large and small missions of the center on a daily basis. The tutors at Nazareth understand the significance of this. Reflecting on why she chose to participate in the writing center, Tishawna explained that she wanted to "show that a minority school has the capabilities to run a writing center efficiently." The tutors are very proud of being able to parlay their communicative and writing skills into tangible benefits for others; this transfer of knowledge and these shared experiences boost their own confidence and self-esteem. Students are consequently empowered in their own work, especially the student who has become frustrated with failure or who is too shy to ask questions when confused. Working with peers in the nonpunitive, nonthreatening environment of our writing center eases a lot of that strain, enabling more communication and more clarity for both tutor and student.

THE IDEAS BEHIND WRITING CENTERS

Throughout Nazareth's writing center journey, I have often reflected on the degree to which the writing center theory I subscribed to does or does not reflect the realities of a high school writing center. Having tutored in Steve North's writing center at Albany, I reread his landmark essay "The Idea of a Writing Center" (1984). I was struck first and foremost by how North idealistically sold writing center work as meaningful and writing center practitioners as professionals whose work deserves respect. North focused on how lonely and difficult the process of writing can be and how the writing tutor can lend a hand simply by asking the questions that the writers don't think to ask themselves. In the essay and in his class at Albany, North addressed issues of harmful misconceptions about center work. He eschewed the idea of the writing center as a fix-it shop and pointed out the wrongful thinking involved in assuming that writing center staff members are present to take on the work that a professor is willing to cede or doesn't want to do at all. Speaking back to these misconceptions, he wrote, "In short, we are not here to serve, supplement, back up, complement, reinforce, or otherwise be defined by any external curriculum. We are here to talk to writ-ers" (North, 1984, p. 440). North argued that writing center staff members play their own uniquely defined roles with a purpose independent of those of professors and teachers.

As much as I originally wanted to hold fast to North's ideals, I found that working within a high school put me at direct odds with North's framework because, by definition, nearly everything in a high school environment is defined by a set curriculum. As a writing center director and tutor, I have often found myself in a position of supplementing, complementing, and reinforc-ing classroom work. I have also frequently allowed writing center sessions to shift into discussions of grammar when a teacher's comments have focused exclusively on mistakes in that arena.

In 1994, North critiqued his own idealism in "Revisiting' The Idea of a Writing Center.'" He wrote, "I think my essay . . . offered a version of what we do that is . . . very attractive; but one which also . . . presents its own kind of jeopardy" (p. 9). In essence, North invoked the caveat that practitioners should not let the perfect be the enemy of the good: The motivation of a student is often local and immediate. He more deeply grounded his theory in the muddy waters of real life, and in doing so, he provided a model for all of us in the field, giving us permission to double back down the path we've taken if that path is not leading to progress.

I find such reconsidering particularly relevant to my work at Nazareth because the vast majority of 14- to 17-year-old students are more motivated by turning a failing grade into a passing grade and getting teachers and parents off their backs. When done correctly, helping students tackle lower-order concerns, such as grammar errors, can lead them to rethink the higher-order concerns.

Cultural Reproduction

Another writing center theorist I have returned to is Kenneth Bruffee, who has written extensively about the benefits of collaborative learning. Bruffee (2007) explained that collaborative learning can facilitate cultural reproduction. My peer tutors do not work miracles in their sessions. They often do not offer any information that has not already been presented elsewhere to the student. What they do, however, is present the information in a new light, stripped of the intimidation factor that accompanies teacher-to-student interaction. I see this reality on a regular basis at our center. Students who come in frequently lack familiarity with the academic practices that more successful students possess. I have seen moments when a tutor approaches a student's assignment from the angle of, "If I were assigned this paper, what I would do first is . . . ," and then they go on to offer a model of behavior that has worked for them in the hope that the student can or will reproduce that behavior en route to their own success.

> **The tutors' and students' own diversity means that the writing center doesn't present any special cultural challenge that the tutors haven't already negotiated in other avenues of their lives.**

One of the most obvious openings for the cultural reproduction model occurs when English Language Learners (ELLs) or English Speakers of other Languages (ESLs) come in to our center for help. These moments also seem to draw out the most apprehension in my tutors. It's not that my tutors don't want to help the (usually Creole-speaking) ESL students who come to them for help; frankly, it's usually a case that their strong desire to help these students paralyzes them, and they find themselves doubting their own ability to mentor a student who is more fluent in a language with which they are unfamiliar. I take these opportunities to discuss with them the ways in which ESL students are more similar to than different from any "mainstream students" (whatever that means) who might come in for help with writing. I remind the tutors not to forget that our East Flatbush high school is part of a highly diverse Brooklyn community where they themselves are from a variety of backgrounds, as are their classmates, as are their neighbors. The tutors' and students' own diversity means that the writing center doesn't present any special cultural challenge that the tutors haven't already negotiated in other avenues of their lives. This awareness helps the peer tutors, who then find that their main function in tutoring ESL students is to slow down the message that was given too swiftly in class and to serve as a patient partner for decoding academic language. Armed with their own experiences and strategies, tutors rarely find themselves in a position they can't handle.

Bringing the Writing Center into the Classroom

Elizabeth Boquet and Neal Lerner (2008) posited in their essay "Reconsiderations: After the Idea of the Writing Center," that our field can no longer abide by the strict separation between classroom teaching and non-classroom teaching. I find myself agreeing with them more and more. The willingness of peer tutors to see themselves as part of the learning process and to negotiate individual modes of communication that work with individual students is a characteristic of writing center work that I wish could be transferred into more classrooms. There is a monologue going on in most classrooms that shuts out student learners and that costs educators the chance to grow in understanding. The dialogic model used in writing center work is one that could be used to benefit many educational encounters if it were more widely embraced. To that end, Boquet and Lerner stress the value of the writing center as a site rich in opportunity for learning about the everyday literacy practices of our students. It is a venue that they believe more researchers need to turn to in order to answer this question: "What happens when students write?"

> **As diverse student bodies become the rule rather than the exception, writing center work can contribute to the positive development of urban education.**

FINAL THOUGHTS

The third year of Nazareth's peer writing center is well under way, and I find my thoughts turning to the ways in which students learn from one another and how those ways differ from how they learn from me or from my colleagues. I observe the modeling, the joking, the encouraging, and the pushing that goes on in the writing center, and I cannot help but believe more of the same should be taking place in our classrooms. My peer tutors have been able to succeed where I have sometimes failed. I think their practice can become the model. The writing center can become a space for less successful students to find new means of expression while developing more effective academic behaviors. Our figurative space can work to break down the walls that lock many nontraditional students out of meaningful learning. And as diverse student bodies become the rule rather than the exception, writing center work can contribute to the positive development of urban education. It is clear that both tutors and students frequently have transformative experiences in the high school writing center. The idea of a high school writing center has already turned into a reality for many high school students and should continue to be for the millions of students who deserve it.

REFERENCES

Black, L. (1998). *Between talk and teaching: Reconsidering the writing conference.* Logan, UT: Utah State University Press.

Boquet, E., & Lerner, N. (2008). Reconsiderations: After the idea of the writing center. *College English 71*(2), 170–189.

Bruffee, K. (2007). *A short course in writing: Composition, collaborative learning, and constructive reading* (4th ed.). New York: Pearson.

Grimm, N. (1999). *Good intentions: Writing center work for postmodern times.* Portsmouth, NH: Boynton/Cook.

North, S. (1984). The idea of a writing center. *College English 46*, 433–446.

North, S. (1994). Revisiting "The idea of a writing center." *The Writing Center Journal 15*(1), 7–19.

CHAPTER FOUR

Building a Peer Tutoring Program

Andrew Jeter

Currently, I run what is widely believed to be the world's largest peer tutoring program. The program is housed in the Literacy Center of Niles West High School in Skokie, Illinois. In 2005, our school merged our existing Writing Center, Reading Center, and Math Center to create the Literacy Center. This new center was tasked with addressing the critical thinking, reading, and writing needs of all students in all of their classes. Today, we have a program housed in 3,000 square feet of space at the heart of our school's academic community. It is staffed by more than 200 peer tutors and 19 staff members who served 31,119 students in 2010 and more than 110,000 since the center's inception. Because I'm the coordinator of the program, my desk sees a never-ending flurry of memos, requests, board and usage reports, budget concerns, and ideas for potential extension programs. This inexhaustible flow of activity, information, and responsibility leads to daily apologies to my assistant and a feeling that I never seem to get anything finished. It is also a source of total joy.

Together, my tutors and staff and I get to celebrate thousands of academic successes. On one tutee's 38th visit of the year, he is greeted with a hail of confetti. Amir is our 10,000th tutee of the year. I give him a Literacy Center t-shirt and a half-pound gummy bear. Another tutor, Roxie, runs in to tell us that she has gotten into Vanderbilt; the English teacher who helped her with her essay beams like an 18-year-old off on a new adventure. Marcus, another tutor, asks me if he can use his tutoring period to help his marching band colleagues. "For what, how to walk?" I ask him. He smiles back and replies, "Yep." As a member of the marching band and a Literacy Center tutor, Marcus helps the band analyze their performance and create a list of improvements to be tackled.

Fariha tutors 71 students in just 15 days, and I go in search of a trophy worthy of her accomplishment for our center's award ceremony. By year's end, Fariha will have helped 501 students in 1 year. She wins the coveted Titan of Tutoring Award, a spray-painted plastic Godzilla action figure.

These and other achievements point to the invaluable role our Literacy Center plays in the school community. But a lot goes on behind the scenes. In this chapter, I want to give readers an overview of what I had to do to start the peer tutoring program that provides the foundation for our success. For the reader who does not have a center, this chapter may act as a guide for what is possible. For the more initiated director or coordinator, I offer my story for consideration of changes that could be made to expand, enliven, or enrich an existing center. To help readers get started, I offer a "to do" list with every section.

DEFINING OUR MISSION

By the fall of 2004, teachers from across the disciplines started to recognize that although our school was studded with boutique programs for students at risk, we had no real place where *any* student could seek assistance. This is when my faculty colleagues and I envisioned combining our existing centers. We knew these centers were primarily addressing the skills that were being taught by the teachers of those departments and, consequently, were more focused on the skills the teachers felt the students needed rather than on students' overall ability to use critical thinking to solve *any* problem they encountered in their academic work. When we combined our math, writing, and reading centers into one, we sought a wider, more generous focus for our new Literacy Center. We also knew that the best way to get students to use the new center was to get them excited and energized about it. In order to do that, we knew we would have to use peer tutors to secure student buy-in, which was critical for students to see that the place really did belong to them. In the end, we envisioned a one-stop-shopping concept guided by Lao Tzu's proverb: "Give a man a fish and you feed him for a day; teach a man to fish and you feed him for a lifetime."

> **We made the decision that the center needed a mission statement that would guide its work, communicate its purpose to the school community, and, at the same time, protect its peer tutors.**

When we first conceived the idea of creating a Literacy Center in our school, we knew that it had one potentially devastating flaw: It could be all things to all people. This is also, ironically, its greatest strength. The Literacy

Center is designed to address the unique needs of each student who walks through its doors. But for the teachers who set out to construct the place, we knew that other teachers, administrators, and parents could potentially perceive this flexibility as a panacea for things that were neither about students nor in their best interest. We foresaw that adults particularly would seek to manipulate the center so that it became a place that solved *all* the problems of our institution. We made the decision, then, that the center needed a mission statement that would guide its work, communicate its purpose to the school community, and, at the same time, protect its peer tutors. Here is a core piece of our mission: Housed in an environment that is friendly to both students and teachers, the Literacy Center promotes a school climate that celebrates and values academic rigor by providing:

- highly competent help in the three core literacies;
- the safety to ask questions;
- a community based on volunteerism and collaboration;
- a common vocabulary for learning about literacy;
- pedagogical practices that link learning disciplines; and
- a shared goal of fostering both rigor and student academic independence and maturity.

Not long after we opened the new Literacy Center, this mission helped us when the disciplinary deans asked us to set aside a table in the center for students assigned to in-school suspension. They wanted to send students to sit at the table, and we would help them during their suspension period(s). Without our mission, we might have ended up with such a mandatory table. Instead, I explained that our mission was to provide "a community based on volunteerism and collaboration" and that a set-aside table of students who had no choice went against that mission. Although the deans were not pleased, we found another way to accommodate them that did not go against our mission and proved to be a better solution for all concerned: Students could self-select to come to the center for academic assistance during in-school suspension.

The importance of a mission cannot be understated. It should direct the daily life and work of the peer tutors and the program. It should protect and nurture peer tutors and provide them with the flexibility they require to meet the ever-changing needs of students. It was a combination of this need for flexibility and wariness about the ability of teachers to reach consensus with something like a mission statement that prompted us to adopt an *evolving* mission statement. With an annual review of our mission, we continue to address the current needs of our students and gain greater buy-in from teachers who are not put off by a monolithic statement.

Getting Started

- Identify stakeholders—those who have a vested interest in the school's center.

- Invite all stakeholders to draft an evolving mission statement by determining what the core philosophy of the center should be.

- Think about who will be served by the center and what their needs are.

- Decide what the center will do and what it will not do.

- Ask stakeholders to reconvene on a regular basis to revise the mission predicated on the needs of students.

- Widely publish the mission statement in the school, the school's publications and announcements, and across the school community.

SELECTING AND EDUCATING OUR TUTORS

During the tutor selection process, we look first for students who are school leaders or potential leaders. This means that we not only seek recommendations from the teachers but also recruit heavily from the volleyball team and the football team. We talk to the choir director, the break dance club sponsor, the chess team sponsor, and the head custodian. Our approach ensures that we have a tutor corps that is naturally inclined to help and to lead. We are also guaranteed a group of peer tutors who rely on their wide and rich diversity of literacy experiences to help other students solve problems and approach difficult academic issues in myriad ways. Combined with a tutor education program that trains students how to ask pertinent questions, listen closely, and serve as a practice audience, a corps of tutors with diverse literacy experiences and learning strategies becomes the perfect solution for assisting a student body with diverse learning needs (see Appendix A).

Once a tutor has been recommended, we invite him or her in for an interview with one of our staff members. We have also found that experienced third-year tutors can make excellent decisions about who will make a good tutor (see Appendix B). After the interview, students who have been recommended by the interviewer to proceed are added to a list that is sent out electronically to the entire staff for their review and comments. The center's teacher staff reviews those comments, and a final decision is made about the candidates. Students who are accepted are sent a contract that they must read and sign before becoming a tutor (see Appendix C). Like our mission, our hiring process is frequently reviewed and revised when appropriate.

Choosing Peer Tutors

- Determine the process by which students will be accepted as tutors for the center.

- Create a database of adults who could recommend students to be tutors and draft an invitation to recommend students with a reminder of the mission of the center, criteria for choosing tutors (see Appendix A), and space to write in names with comments.

- Draft a congratulatory letter for students who were recommended. This letter can also be an invitation to come in for an interview if that is a part of the tutor selection process.

- Draft a contract for the tutors to sign that is linked to the mission statement.

- Create an interview form if needed.

- Consider sending out a list of the potential candidates for teacher review.

- Draft final letters of acceptance and denial. (We have used our denial letters to encourage students to volunteer elsewhere in the community.)

TRAINING OUR TUTORS

After a rather unsuccessful attempt to *teach* students how to tutor, we took a step back and decided to see what they were actually doing when they tutored their peers. We observed their sessions and created a training guide based on those sessions we deemed successful. Surprisingly, we learned that what our tutors were using, again and again, was essentially the ubiquitous Think-Aloud strategy used by reading teachers across the country. Our experienced tutors were using this strategy liberally for all manner of work, from assisting with a freshman essay to explaining a physics problem. Tutors gave voice to what they thought as they read a text, worked through a computation, made a decision, or organized information. In this way, the tutee heard what the tutor, or practice audience, thought while engaging their text, writing, or assignment. In doing so, tutors also modeled academic maturity, or the ability to self-navigate through the strategies needed to be successful in school.

From these observations, we devised a six-step guide to tutoring:

1. Setting Purpose
2. Getting to Know the Assignment
3. Visualizing Information
4. Asking Questions
5. Making the Invisible Visible (Expressing the Tutor's Thoughts Aloud)
6. Allowing the Tutee to Learn by Working

Because these steps capture teenagers' approach to problem solving, the training allows tutors to use the language that students use rather than the educational jargon of teachers. By using this simple guide, we effectively train our tutors in a short, 1-day summer orientation and then return to the guide during the tutors' regularly scheduled tutoring shifts.

On the 1-day summer orientation day, new tutors are broken up into groups of approximately 20. The groups are led by two or three seasoned, senior tutors who take the morning to explain and model the six steps. The afternoon is filled with activities that help the new tutors understand their role as leaders in our school. Each group also has at least one teacher present who can step in to explain expectations, if there is uncertainty. These same teachers are then present in the center to work with the tutors over the course of the year. This ongoing training occurs primarily through observations and discussions about tutoring sessions and the six-step guide.

Training Peer Tutors

- Determine what is important for tutors to know.
- Craft or find a guide for educating tutors. (Many books are available on tutor training.)
- Determine the following:
  » When will tutors be trained?
  » Where will tutors be trained?
- Once tutor orientation has happened:
  » Take time to review what happened.
  » Determine whether or not it had the desired outcome.
  » Survey the tutors to determine what they remember and what they use.
- Start planning next year's orientation immediately after the current orientation ends.

EVALUATING THE PEER TUTORING PROGRAM

Structured Conversations

For several years, the teachers in our center prepared quarterly performance evaluations of our tutors. Although the rationale behind these evaluations was to improve tutors' tutoring abilities, we found that our tutors viewed the evaluations as a kind of high-stakes test. We quickly moved to change that perception. We renamed our evaluations *structured conversations* and linked them, point by point, to our tutoring guide and the Think-Aloud strategy. We have worked to ensure that all tutors understand that the structured conversations are not our way of finding fault with them but instead are about improving their skills as tutors. The structured conversation is a simple process, really, wherein a teacher observes a tutor during a session and then talks with the tutor about how the session went. Together, they decide what steps the tutor can take in the future to appropriately engage tutees.

We have found that tutors actually enjoy these conversations. In year-end reflections, tutors have shared that these structured conversations helped them hone their tutoring skills and more deeply appreciate the intricacies of their work. They learned to look at these structured conversations not as tutor remediation but as ways to strengthen our learning community. We came to realize that although we championed a peer-to-peer model, we could learn even more about tutoring if we allowed our tutors to observe their peers for these structured conversations. As a result, seasoned tutors also observe their peers. The resultant conversations are astounding. Tutors talking together about the intricacies of their work reveals the inherent power of peer collaboration.

Tutee Evaluations

Another way we determine whether our peer tutoring program meets our goals is by surveying our tutees. We feel strongly that since the center was constructed for our students, they ought to have a say in how it is assessed. Every year during the first week in December, we distribute a satisfaction survey to tutees at the end of their tutoring sessions. We also give them space to write their thoughts and concerns. Each year, students return approximately 200 surveys that provide us with a glimpse into the minds of the students who use our center.

We attempt to measure our effectiveness in tutoring students in other ways as well. We use blind, holistic scoring of essays before and after a visit to the center. We provide reading inventories to tutees before and after one-on-one reading assistance. We also track the relationship between visits to the center for study skills assistance, principally for vocabulary and test scores in that area.

Evaluating Tutees

- Use the training material that is used during tutor orientation to evaluate tutors' work during sessions.

- Create an evaluation form that informs the observers what to look for in the observation. Share this with tutors.

- Create a timetable for observing tutors during the year.

- Hold tutors accountable for their observations and the conversations they create.

- Keep in mind that tutor observations are best when they are focused on helping the tutors become better tutors.

ENLIVENING THE LITERACY CULTURE OF OUR SCHOOL: MAKING IT FUN FOR STUDENTS

As important as tutor selection, education, and evaluations are, tutors will get lonely if tutees do not come in for help. For this reason, it is vitally important that a center be a welcoming place where students understand that although they will be engaged in academic work, the space should be fun, interesting, and engaging. By paying close attention to the physical space of the center and the ways in which the program advertises itself and celebrates its tutors, a director can show how a peer tutoring program can have a significant impact on the literacy culture of a school.

Physical Space

During one of our first design meetings, it was suggested that bean-bag chairs might make students feel more comfortable about coming to the Literacy Center. Never mind that the average American teenager does not have a beanbag chair at home, we felt that teenagers slouching around on the floor would not send the kind of message we wanted to promote; our mission statement told us that we were to be "friendly to both students and teachers" and that we should be fostering both "academic rigor" and "maturity." Somehow, we could not imagine most of our staff feeling comfortable, or our students being able to focus on the tough work of high school, while lolling around in beanbag chairs.

Today, our center is furnished with 102 plastic chairs and tables. The rest of the space exudes comfort while celebrating multiple literacy successes.

Our annual t-shirt designs are respectfully retired, framed, and hung about the space. A dozen living, hardy plants hang from the ceiling. A potpourri of photographs of former tutors and tutees covers most of the walls. One wall is dedicated to the Fine Arts department and students' art. Another wall is taken up entirely by a bulletin board devoted to tutors' and tutees' successes throughout the school community. Our patio, in the school courtyard, is open to students who do not have to ask permission to use it for tutoring. Our center is designed to be the tutors' and tutees' place, where they can be recognized and empowered. Even without beanbag chairs or sofas, tutors love being there because we have made it a place that honors them for being great leaders, great students, and just great teenagers.

Competitions

Because our mission recognizes the importance of student buy-in, another way to get students to see coming to the Literacy Center as worthwhile and fun is to run competitions that are quick, easy to participate in, and hold the promise of an unusual prize. Any competition should require no more than 5 minutes from students. After all, they are in the center to do academic work, and they become quite wary of wasting time. Speed-story writing, six-word memoirs, and equation-solving competitions can be completed at the end of a tutoring session and engage students in work that builds on disciplinary content without making it the "same old thing."

> **It is vitally important that a center be a welcoming place where students understand that although they will be engaged in academic work, the space should be fun, interesting, and engaging.**

Awarding the prizes for these competitions is also a great way to get the center out into the classrooms. We often wait to determine the winners. Then we ask one of the winner's teachers if we can come to award the student at the beginning of that class. We take confetti and the prize and make a celebration of it. We have delivered prizes to chemistry classes, algebra classes, and technical drawing classes, and each time, we have made an impact on each student in the room like no flyer or handout could. We also recognize our 10,000th, 20,000th, and 30,000th tutee of the year this way.

The prizes we deliver also send a message, so we eschew the prizes that are expected: no pretty journals or nice pens here. We know that teenagers love t-shirts and food. So we give away burritos, boxes of Halloween cereal, homemade lunches, stacks of pancakes, and half-pound and 5-pound gummy bears. To our 100,000th tutee, we delivered 100 *100 Grand* candy bars. In our school, the students know that if they see their friend with a gummy bear the size of a small child, that friend has probably been to the Literacy Center. Word gets around.

Celebrating Peer Tutors

High school peer tutors provide an invaluable service for which they are rarely appropriately compensated. Thus, we wanted to offer our tutors one half-credit per semester. Rewarding tutors with credits costs the school nothing, and the benefits are priceless. The credits appear on the tutors' transcripts. None of them needs the credit, so most frequently fail to realize that they earn it. But recognition is necessary for the tutors and the school community. Recognition reminds everyone what an amazing job peer tutors do and how important they are to enriching the community's literacy learning. It is the peer tutoring program at our school that is largely responsible for increased recognition and embracing of academic rigor in the past few years. This must be recognized and celebrated.

We also recognize our tutors by awarding them school-color cords to be worn at graduation. In the program, we list and recognize tutors as community leaders. We have created the National Peer Tutor Honor Society and have made the cords an acknowledgment of their membership in that organization. Early on, we also arranged to award our tutors at the all-school Accolades ceremony. The ceremony is quite a lengthy affair, as it honors students for a wide array of school programs and activities. The center was given one award that became our Tutor of the Year Award. Although that award is wonderful, we knew it was not enough. We created the Literacy Center Award Ceremony, which is now firmly ensconced on the school calendar. At our own ceremony in late May, we give out awards by year and by department, which also promotes buy-in from the teachers of those departments. We award tutors for being extraordinary journeymen and outstanding leaders. We have a Renaissance Tutor Award for the tutor most flexible in their tutoring and a Golden Pencil Sharpener Award for most tutees served. The pencil sharpener is real, it works, and many tutors have taken it with them to college. And this year, because of Fariha's incredible feat of tutoring 501 students in one year, I spray-painted a 12-inch Godzilla action figure, had it mounted on a plaque, and presented it as the Incredible, Unstoppable Titan of Tutoring Award.

At the award ceremony, we also honor our Frequent Flyers, our repeat customers who come so frequently we know when they are sick, in trouble, or celebrating a birthday. They are as much a part of our center as our tutors and teachers. And we honor all of the tutors who have assisted more than 100 tutees over the course of the year. They get medallions and plastic Roman centurion helmets because we call them Centurions. They are the elite within the elite. They are so dedicated that they come in for extra shifts or walk in with people whom they have recognized as needing a little help out in the school. As these tutors reach their 100th tutee, we put their pictures up on the bulletin board, which makes their fellow tutors try harder to earn that honor.

We also use a bulletin board outside the center's door to post the names of students who have been recommended as tutors for the forthcoming year. As they come in for their interviews, we check off their names. During passing periods, students stop and discuss the candidates and their progress through the hiring process. Once the selections have been made, a new list is posted under a banner that reads "Your Tutors for Next Year." Students stop and discuss, setting the school abuzz with talk of what next year will be like and who will be missed once they graduate.

Inside the center, on another bulletin board, we display the pictures of our tutors of the month, our tutors on teams and clubs, and our tutors who have been recognized elsewhere in the school community. We post their pictures again and again, at track meets, basketball games, math competitions, and pep rallies. We promote our tutors because they deserve it, and because other students realize how great our tutors are. It makes students want to work with their peers, not because they are smart or pretty, but because they are out there, taking risks, trying new things, and having fun.

Promoting the Center

- Create a list of all of the existing ways that students are recognized in the school community and a list of promotions that other organizations in the school (library, clubs, teams, and so on) use regularly.

- Brainstorm other ways that recognition could happen in the school.

- Brainstorm a list of alternative ways that the center could be promoted.

- Contact centers in other areas to ask what they do.

- Use the brainstorm lists to create annual recognitions and promotions that are unique and surprising.

- Always remember that the work of the center is to recognize and focus on students. This will keep promotions and celebrations about students and remind them that they are valued.

FINAL THOUGHTS

Nikki tutored math in English and Spanish, Arnold played card tricks, Sam liked to give social tips to freshman boys, Boris sounded like the neighborhood curmudgeon, and Esther was the captain of the girls' volleyball and basketball teams. Each of them was an incredible tutor who reached hundreds of young people in the years they worked in our Literacy Center. In many ways, their successes had to do with their drive to help others. This is one benefit that the Literacy Center has brought to our school. By developing a tutor education program based on tutors' strengths and talents, and by allowing those tutors to feel ownership over their center, we have nurtured in our students an understanding that we respect them.

> **By developing a tutor education program based on tutors' strengths and talents, and by allowing those tutors to feel ownership over their center, we have nurtured in our students an understanding that we respect them.**

Another major benefit comes from when students meet with the tutors. They find greater, more readily available success in the classroom and with the tasks given them. With this success, school has become an easier, more enjoyable place to be. When students enjoy school more, they allow themselves to feel ownership of the school and pride in their community. Peer tutoring is about modeling academic maturity, and when a school is full of academically mature students, everyone is happy and successful.

Finally, our program has also served as a reminder that the work of strengthening student literacy skills and of building high-quality educational programs is recursive work. Over and over, from our mission statement to our forms and approaches, our team of teachers reviews what has been done and revises our plans for the future. This allows our program to appropriately reflect the literacy needs of our ever-changing student body. Constant reflection allows our program to grow and mature. Dedicating a school's resources to this type of program will enable students, teachers, and the community to have an active role in nurturing the academic success of all students.

CHAPTER FIVE

Revising and Rewriting Roles

Exploring the Challenges of Peer Tutors in a High School Writing Center

Cynthia Dean

"Writing center? What's that?"

That was the reaction of three students who were with me at a summer state conference to present their work in multi-genre research. Since we had some time before our workshop, I asked these three students to go to Rich Kent's workshop on creating student-staffed writing centers.

Approximately 25 teachers attended the workshop; my high school students were the only young people there. They were, however, active participants who asked questions in the small-group conversations and offered their student viewpoints. Sally, one of the veteran members of my presentation team, said, "*This* is a great idea, but we'll have more trouble convincing the teachers than the students." On the way home, the three students could not stop talking about "how cool" a writing center would be.

Over the next semester, I worked closely with Richard Kent (2006), the author of *Creating Student-Staffed Writing Centers, grades 6–12*, to learn about writing center policy and philosophy. Through my observations of writing classrooms in the school in which I work, I had come to the conclusion that writing is mostly an isolating act. Teachers assign; students write; teachers assess. Moving beyond this mode of writing and writing instruction in schools is often hampered by the structure of coverage-laden curriculum that prevents teachers from providing authentic and useful feedback on student writing. Teachers simply don't have time. I knew from my work with Rich that one possible way to address this problem was through the use of writing centers staffed by peer tutors. Students helping students and providing feedback to one another can supplement teacher feedback and provide a new and exciting audience for student work.

With administrative approval, a small grant, and 27 peer tutors who had completed afterschool sessions to learn about collaborative peer tutoring, the writing center opened at the end of January 2007. I learned a great deal that semester about scheduling, student and teacher buy-in, and tutor angst. Most important, I realized that students needed more support for their work in the writing center. Four weeks of afterschool sessions on learning how to be a collaborative tutor was not enough. It became clear to me that I needed to offer a formal course in which student tutors could share experiences and in which their own writing could be nurtured. From this understanding, our Writing Center English course was conceived.

THE DELICATE ROLE OF A PEER TUTOR

As the writing center director and course instructor, I provided these students with materials that oriented them to collaborative learning, provided a forum for tutor practice and role-play, supported their writing, and allowed them to share and learn from tutoring stories. The students exceeded my expectations. They spoke about their successes and challenges, they shared writing, and they taught one another how to be collaborative tutors. As I watched these young people grow as learners and tutors, I realized that they were more than just students who worked in a writing center; they were becoming authorities on being a writing tutor and growing in ways that I had not anticipated. Sean, a peer tutor from the inception of the center, crystallized this growth for me:

> **It is our duty and call to aid writers, not to sit idle. And in order to "do our job" we need to be prepared.**

> As tutors of the writing center, we need to be firmly aware that we are not experts. We have as much to learn from the student as the student does from us. The moment we begin to patronize the students is the moment they tune us out; we're just another teacher and a waste of their time. So I caution myself and my peers to understand the center and its purpose. Not only to understand but to advocate for this purpose—this center for writing. It is our duty and call to aid writers, not to sit idle. And in order to "do our job," we need to be prepared.

The mature and thoughtful nature of these words could have come from a teacher, but they came from a 17-year-old. The other tutors echoed Sean's sentiments. Amazed and pleased at the level of expertise, knowledge, and reflection these students exhibited, I also realized that perhaps their tutorial role might be causing some problems in their everyday school lives. I began to anticipate that, for some teachers, tutors' advocacy of their collaborative work might not be welcome in the classroom. Even though the tutors were enacting roles they valued, these roles were not always viewed as appropriate in other classes where students generally were expected to view the teacher as the sole authority and where participation and work were tightly controlled.

My main interest as a teacher-researcher, therefore, was documenting tutors' perceptions of their transition from student-writer to student-tutor in order to better understand the challenges they faced. How, in their role as tutors, were my students' perceptions of writing and writing instruction altered? Did my students distinguish between teaching and tutoring, and if so, how? Finally, I wanted to know what influence, if any, their tutorial identities had on those they enacted in conventional classrooms.

I began by collecting observational field notes and material artifacts that illuminated the practices and personalities of the nine peer tutors enrolled in the tutor preparation course. After this initial phase of data collection, I decided to limit my focus to four tutors.

As I investigated the challenges that students face as they transition from their identities as writers to the identities of tutors, I found three key themes. First, I discovered that the previous writing histories of these tutors influenced the ways in which they enacted their tutorial identity. The second theme arose as tutors articulated and enacted their tutorial identities. They resisted the traditional authority associated with teaching and insisted that tutoring and teaching were distinct and different. Third, in assuming a tutorial identity, these tutors reported changing relationships with teachers.

Revisiting Writing Histories

I asked the students to talk about their writer identity in order to better understand how their histories may have influenced their identities as tutors. Often, students have been influenced by past educational experiences—sometimes positive, sometimes negative—and in order to understand their current perspectives, it is essential to understand where they are coming from. In the process of revisiting their writing histories, tutors revealed both pleasant and unpleasant experiences. With writers I had noticed that after a trimester of participating in the course and tutoring in the writing center, tutors' perceptions of writing and writing instruction seemed to be changing.

Sally, a second-year tutor, presents a writing history in which she marks growth as a writer but also presents a background dominated by teacher-assigned writing. She does, however, offer a few instances where she was not constrained by the teacher but instead was encouraged to write in ways that emphasized the skills and genres that she enjoyed. For example, she reports that in her sophomore-year English class, she was able to choose topics and genres for her writing that were still within the parameters of the assignment. She credited this experience with helping her to become a more confident writer. For the most part, however, Sally expressed frustration with rigid formats and limited topics.

> We didn't write about anything we wanted to. It was all things they told us to write about with a rubric . . . which I *absolutely hate.* And I guess it's necessary, but . . . it's just I can't stand it. I'm so used to dealing with rubrics and having a specific way that things are supposed to be done that I find it difficult to free write anymore. I try to see the teacher's point of view; teachers are used to the five-paragraph essay, and I think that it would be a very hard transition for them to make [to student choice]. A teacher might be scared that they're losing some sort of control.

Sally conveys her distaste for the specific demands of a rubric and the lack of topic choice. Interestingly, despite her protest, in the next breath she acknowledges rubrics and teacher-driven assignments as somehow necessary to enact authority in the classroom. Sally associated the five-paragraph essay, the quintessential formula for writing, as a vehicle for teachers to control students and student writing. She laments that because of specificity, she struggles to "free write" anymore. Being forced to write in teacher-led ways created a dilemma for Sally. She had to comply with assignments in order to succeed in school, but in complying, she was losing her ability to write freely.

Abby's history was a counterpoint to Sally's, who generally reported a school writing history that was teacher-led. Abby, a high-honors student in her first year of tutoring, described an early school writing history where a teacher offered coaching and guidance in the writing process instead of directives and corrections. When I asked her to talk about her history as a writer, she immediately recalled her third-grade experience, where her teacher fostered a culture of writing.

> When I was in third grade, my teacher would read us *Little House on the Prairie.* . . . [I]t was just inspirational. She would read, and we wrote. I have all these stories that I wrote that year in this book, three or four composition notebooks, with all these stories about my classmates. I really started to like writing in the little world I could have that was kind of like Laura's [Laura Ingalls Wilder's], and I could just write, and it could just be free and full of anything that I wanted it to be. I just kept writing and writing.

In contrast to Sally's lack of choice and the procedural demands in school writing situations, Abby's third-grade experience was one of relative freedom. Abby implied that because of this experience, she grew to love writing. In Sally's case, the experience of tightly regulated writing restricted and impaired her ability to write.

Abby's experience with an unconventional context for writing might relate in some way to her capacity to imagine alternative models of writing instruction. Interestingly, when I asked tutors to describe what the best way to teach writing might be, Abby appeared most insistent that there has to be a balance between learning academic forms and writing expressively.

> I have seen a classroom where everyone bounces ideas off of each other and learns different approaches to writing, [where] there is not just one way to produce a good piece of writing. I have, however, also seen the side where everything is structured and a specific way is expected with little or no exceptions. . . . [B]oth work for me and I believe this enables me to see the good and bad of them. We don't have to go one way or another. We don't have to stick completely to the conventional ways of teaching writing, and we don't have to completely do away with it. There is some common ground; it just needs to be found. And I think that will start when we realize that in writing, everyone has their own style, and there is nothing wrong with that. The teacher's job should be to help students find the way that works best for them, not to force-feed them one way for 12 years.

Abby has been successful in both teacher-centered and student-centered classrooms, yet she advocated for a balance where conventional academic writing and personal style are not seen as separate skills. Her personal history seemed to position her to understand the diversity in writing instruction while still advocating for an alternate paradigm of writing instruction.

Sally's and Abby's writing histories revealed much about the mindset they brought to tutoring and writing. What became clear for me was that their experiences in classrooms had vividly shaped their memories of what it means to teach writing.

Defining a Tutor's Authority

Another theme that surfaced was the ways in which the students defined and enacted their roles as tutors. Nadine and Ashley are both second-year tutors who insist that teaching and tutoring are different constructs. Each describes and contextualizes her role as tutor in the school.

Nadine summed up the tutors' shared assessment of what teachers do: "Teachers stand up in front of you and lecture you for like an hour and here's your homework, now do it. That's what I've always gotten." Here, Nadine is clear about the nature and function of teacher authority in her experience. Being a tutor, therefore, involved a profound change in how authority is enacted. The collaborative nature of tutoring and what Nadine sees as authoritative teaching are polar opposites. To Nadine, the teacher is the one with the most knowledge, experience, and authority, and therefore is the one to deliver information or directions. Nadine reports that because she is a student, is less experienced, and has little authority, the notion that she could be a teacher just doesn't work for her. Yet, in assuming a tutorial identity, she assumed authority, even if she doesn't articulate it as an authoritative role. For Nadine, legitimate authority seemed reciprocal; she described her tutoring as a kind of give-and-take that is almost playful:

> **Being a tutor, therefore, involved a profound change in how authority is enacted. The collaborative nature of tutoring and what Nadine sees as authoritative teaching are polar opposites.**

> I think tutoring is more one-on-one. They'll [student-writers] give you something, and you'll give something back. It's kind of give-and-take. That's the only way to learn. We'll look at the paper in chunks as opposed to going over the whole paper because they get overwhelmed. I'll ask them to read it and say, "What did you think of that? Does it sound right to you?" It's kind of putting it back on them and they come up with the coolest ideas. Conversation just opens them up.

Nadine understood her role as a guide to orient students to manageable amounts of material. Providing the context students need to share their writing comfortably and shifting responsibility for revision to the client by using a questioning strategy are qualities that Nadine enacted in her tutorial identity. While she assumed authority for guiding the client, she resisted the directive authority she associated with teaching.

Ashley described her typical tutorial in a slightly different way. Instead of micro-focusing on pieces of the paper, as Nadine appeared to do, Ashley adopted a wider view of her tutorial role. Like Nadine, she oriented her clients to the tutorial but did so in a more holistic manner.

> I'd introduce myself and get a feel for their paper. Then I'd ask the student to figure out the most important things that they want to work on. So sort of like formulate a list of things that they want to work on and change in their paper and take it by priority for the student and

then check it off as we go, and when we've gone through the whole list, we go back through it one more time to see that the student likes how it is and then send them off, knowing if they find something else later on, they can always come back.

Ashley enacted her tutorial identity in a more structured way than Nadine. For Ashley, there seemed to be a need to be more organized and purposeful. Instead of chunking the material and going through it piece by piece like Nadine, Ashley created a list to address with the client that was covered at least twice. While the tutee prioritized the list, it was Ashley who organized the direction of the tutorial and facilitated the dialogue. Ashley, more than Nadine, seemed to be assuming the mantle of expert in her tutorials. While Nadine and Ashley both embraced collaborative learning and teaching, each enacted her tutorial identity in a different way.

In defining themselves as tutors, Nadine and Ashley wished to distance themselves from the definition that associated what they did with teacher-like authority. They both, however, reported interactions with teacher authority that helped me to further understand how they distinguished tutoring from teaching. Nadine reported an occasion where she did not understand or agree with the procedural demands a writer's teacher had imposed.

I went to the teacher so I could understand what [they] wanted because [the writer is] sitting there telling me, and I didn't understand. I would do it [differently] and if that's not what the teacher wants, I don't want to get the student in trouble. So I asked that teacher, "What do you want? What do you mean by this?" I felt like I was kind of pushing in on [their] territory but if I understand it, I can help [the writer].

Nadine's conference with the teacher was a key moment in shaping her tutorial identity. Nadine understood that, as a tutor, she had authority only to help her tutee within the parameters of the assignment. In order to clarify the assignment, Nadine went to the teacher while she had the tutee wait in the writing center. Despite her disagreement with the way the teacher had structured the assignment, Nadine felt it was her duty to seek clarification immediately. Even though she reported that approaching the teacher was somewhat uncomfortable, she felt secure enough in her tutorial identity to exert her tutorial authority. Within the writing center, tutors have the authority to shape and guide tutorials. Outside the writing center, however, is where teacher authority is enacted. What is most interesting here in terms of tutorial authority is that, although Nadine reported that she was unsure of how the teacher would receive her request for clarification, her uneasiness did not stop her. In this case, tutor authority and teacher authority did not result in any kind of disagreement. Rather, Nadine indicated that the teacher was happy to discuss the assignment and thanked her for seeking her out.

Ashley, like Nadine, was at a place in her own self-definition where she felt equipped to exert her tutorial authority. When I asked her about interactions with teachers in regard to her status as a tutor, Ashley shared her concerns about her teachers' understanding of her work. When a teacher's definition of what it means to tutor contrasted with her own, she did not hesitate to correct him.

> I told Mr. Bond, "No, it's not. It's not [a place] where they [the students] are going to come in, and we're going to mark up their paper and send them off. It's a place where we nurture the student, not the paper." And I think that a lot of teachers have a really hard time understanding because they think, "How can you nurture the student without nurturing the paper?" I think they're starting to figure it out the more we're around, but still it's a work in progress.

Ashley expresses deep concern for the mind-set of some teachers and offers the example of Mr. Bond to sum up teacher perceptions of tutoring. Instead of accepting the usual authority of a teacher, however, Ashley felt qualified to correct his misconception. In saying "no" to a teacher, Ashley was challenging a definition of tutoring grounded in product instead of process. Ashley seemed to believe that redefining writing in terms of the writer instead of the actual writing is not something that conventional teachers would understand without assistance. Her words—"figure it out"—suggests that one role of tutors is to educate teachers about collaborative processes. Ashley's term "a work in progress" seems a good way to describe how the roles of teacher and tutor continue to be revised.

According to Ashley's and Nadine's reports, tutors were not only orienting tutees to the collaborative nature of their work, but they were assisting teachers in rearticulating what it means to teach and tutor collaboratively.

Reinventing Relationships

One of the questions I sought answers to was whether peer tutors encountered relational challenges as they moved from being a tutor to being a student. I asked students to describe if and how their relationships with their teachers might have changed since the onset of their work as tutors. All four reported they experienced some changes. Here, I recount two tutors' experiences.

Abby related both positive and negative relationships with her teachers. While she reported that some teachers supported her work, she also talked of teachers who seemed to be threatened by her assumption of "teacher" roles. Abby indicated that when a teacher did not support or understand her tutorial work, she worried about maintaining a classroom relationship with the teacher but also felt she had to defend her work.

"That's great. Working together is great." That was actually a math teacher that said that, so it was nice that [a teacher] said that, but on the other side there are teachers that think the writing center isn't very helpful, and because they're a teacher they know better. . . . [S]ometimes I think you can tell that there is a friction when the subject comes up. It's like we shouldn't think in a way that we're able to do this, like they're the only ones that can help and they know better and that students aren't good enough to help other students.

Abby appreciated her math teacher's support and the understanding of the collaborative work enacted in the writing center. The other teachers Abby described, however, seemed to believe tutors were overstepping their bounds as students when they responded to student work or offered revisionary advice to writers. She felt that at least one of her teachers felt "we shouldn't think in a way that we're able to do this." Abby's words suggest that the teacher's comments were directed at her in order to inhibit her tutorial authority. In one of the focus-group interviews, Abby indicated that she felt that sometimes she had to defend the writing center to certain teachers but also had to do so in a way that did not offend the teacher. Abby's status as a high-honors student in combination with her sense of empowerment garnered from writing center involvement may have complicated her relationship with those teachers who were insistent on a teacher-centered classroom.

> **In saying "no" to a teacher, Ashley was challenging a definition of tutoring grounded in product instead of process.**

Negotiating and navigating teacher perceptions of what it means to be a tutor created tensions for Sally as well. Sally felt that at least one teacher, when she became aware of Sally's tutorial identity, expected more from her. Sally felt pressured to perform at increasingly high levels because of this expectation. In my observations during my 3-year relationship with Sally, I have come to know her as the kind of student who needs encouragement for and acknowledgment of her writing. Her tutorial identity has assisted her in gaining self-confidence, but from her report, it appears that her identity as a tutor has also created some problems for her in terms of teacher expectations.

With Mrs. Maoury, I think she looks at me in a different light now . . . it kind of feels like she's expecting more from me out of my papers. . . . I just wrote a paper [for her] and I got a really good grade on it. She wrote a comment like "How come you haven't written like this all year?"

The implication here is that because of her tutorial identity, Sally was expected to write at significantly higher levels than other students. There seemed to be a perception on the part of this teacher that tutoring expertise equals expert, flawless writing. Sally related that although she loves to write, she doesn't always write perfectly, as evidenced by Mrs. Maoury's comment. Sally felt that her work in the writing center had improved her writing, but she also felt that, given her tutorial identity, the expectations of teachers sometimes were unreasonable.

Abby and Sally both experienced tensions as they sought to reconcile their tutorial identities with their student identities in their respective classrooms. Their relationships with some teachers and those teachers' perceptions of their identities most certainly shifted because of their tutoring activities.

FINAL THOUGHTS

I embarked on this path of inquiry to understand and document the challenges high school writing tutors encountered as they transitioned between being student-writers and being peer tutors. Tutors reflected on their writing histories, shared their changing perceptions of writing and writing instruction, and related their stories of what it means to assume, shape, and enact tutorial identity and authority.

Through their tutoring and their experience in the writing center course, tutors enacted a student-centered learning climate and were able to reflect deeply about their roles as tutors and writers. In describing their work as tutors, they eschewed the label of "teacher" because, in their experience, teaching was associated with directives and control. Because of their understanding and experience with collaborative work, transitioning back and forth between the writing center and directive classrooms complicated their school lives.

Since I focused on a small group of tutors, I cannot generalize that the experiences of these tutors will apply to all high school tutors. I do, however, believe that the stories of these peer tutors highlight a need to provide high school writing tutors with a context for examining not just their identities as tutors but also their performative challenges as they transition between writing and tutoring. Although I did not set out to document how the writing center course influenced the capacity of students to reflect on and enact new identities, it became clear that the course played a significant role in assisting tutors to reconcile their tutorial identities with their student identities.

The challenges these students experienced are associated with competing paradigms of teaching and learning, and the course aided them in coming to terms with the tensions they experienced. Peer tutoring interrupts the status quo of teacher authority and suggests that high school writing tutors can be agents of change who introduce and advocate for a less conventional definition of what it means to teach.

REFERENCE

Kent, R. (2006). *Creating student-staffed writing centers, grades 6–12*. New York: Peter Lang.

CHAPTER SIX

The Tutors Speak

Current and Former Tutors' Reflections

Alexandra Elchinoff and Caroline Kowalski

with contributions from current and former tutors:
Hannah Baran, Emma Boel, Jon-Carlos Evans, Jasmyne Grismore,
Allie Grondine, Naba Khan, Stephany Martinez, Justin Schulz, Sarah Senan,
Kendal Shapses, Nicole Wilson, Winta Woldu, and Rachel Wrobel

Oh. . .
by Winta Woldu
Edison High School Tutor and Student

I am a tutor not an editor let me explain it to you.
I am here to assist and help improve your paper too.
Let's take our time and go through your piece,
And I'll prove, with hard work your grade will increase.

Everyone needs help with something they are not too good at. The older generation needs help with learning how to use computers. The parental generation needs help not only raising their kids but also relating to them. Children need help learning to walk, read, and eat. What about teenagers? What do they need help with? Speaking as teenage students from high schools in California and Virginia, one thing we all agree on is that we can improve our writing. Whether we write novels before we start high school or whether we can't bear the thought of writing a three-page essay, we can all use someone to help us improve our written communication skills. Writing centers in our high schools enable us to be able to come in with questions about our essay assignments and leave feeling confident and ready to write or revise. As high school tutor Winta's opening poem illustrates, tutors are able to guide their tutees into writing well-written essays simply by listening and giving advice. The writing center is also a place to meet new people and get guidance for other subjects. Most important, the writing center is a place to feel comfortable not only with yourself but also with your work.

Tutoring is one of the most satisfying acts. In the classroom, we see other students in need of help but do not always know how to help them. By knowing how to tutor, we can help those students improve in their schoolwork while not actually having to do the work for them. Though guidance is a feature of tutoring, the most important aspect is listening. Throughout each session, we keep our tutees talking, and we ask questions that will steer them through whatever assignment they are working on. It is particularly essential to keep this knowledge of tutoring with us because tutoring sessions help both tutors and tutees establish important relationships that benefit them both.

In this chapter, we tutors write about how we first benefited from being tutored in the writing center, before we became tutors ourselves. We were able to get help on our assignments, which in turn made us more confident writers, and often helped us earn better grades. Then, we will reflect on what we have personally gained as tutors. Many students do not ask for help from their teachers because it's scary; getting help from peers is less intimidating and makes asking for help easier. For those who are wondering just how high school students are able to work with student-writers, we will go on to share

> **The writing center is a place to feel comfortable not only with yourself, but also with your work.**

several of our approaches to tutoring. If their first session goes well, tutees are likely to come back to us for help and gain more confidence in their writing. Finally, as three of our co-authors demonstrate, the benefits of tutoring last well beyond high school. They show us that we will carry the experience we gain through tutoring in a high school writing center for the rest of our lives, no matter what path we follow.

HOW TUTEES BENEFIT FROM PEER TUTORING

The main purpose of a peer tutor–based writing center is to benefit tutees. So naturally, the most obvious advantages will be for them. In the following section, we share some of the experiences we had visiting the writing center, which in turn made us want to become tutors. Nicole explains how the equality between tutors and tutees helps tutees feel less intimidated when asking for help. Kendel shares how bouncing ideas off the tutor made the difference in her work. Stephany observes how her writing center experience made her transition from one high school to another easier. Finally, Sarah gives her perspective as a tutee who was able to transfer what she learned in the writing center to all of her writing assignments.

Tutees Seek Help When They Aren't Intimidated—Nicole

If a person has never heard about or experienced peer tutoring, they might ask, "What are the benefits of peer tutoring? Why allow a student to do a teacher's job?" These are questions that are expected from someone who has never experienced peer tutoring. However, these questions stem from a common misconception. A tutor does not have the same job as a teacher. A teacher is an individual who grades and sometimes even edits a student's paper. A tutor is an individual who does not grade or edit a student's paper but assists and guides them to a better understanding of their assignment. A tutor's main goal is not only to help a student on the paper that they are working on but to help them become a better writer.

Often, schools that have successful writing centers have peer tutors. How can peer tutoring be so effective? How can a student helping another student be more effective to a tutee than a teacher helping a student? There is no single reason to answer this question but rather many. One of the main reasons is that a peer tutor is a peer of the tutee. Although this fact is quite obvious, my father, who is a police officer, often says, "Important information that can lead to an answer is often disguised within obvious statements." Since a peer tutor is a peer of the tutee, this can help the tutee feel less intimidated than they would in the same situation with an adult or teacher. For this same reason, there is more of a sense of equality when it comes to authority between a peer tutor and the tutee. Teachers have the power, ultimately, to give grades, whereas tutors do not. So sometimes working with a peer can make the tutee more inclined to think about their improvements, rather than automatically doing them because their teacher told them to. This can also lead the tutee to feel more comfortable in the tutoring session. Creating a comfortable, nonhostile, and hospitable environment can lead to deeper discussion about ideas and work between the tutor and tutee.

Tutees Bounce Ideas off Their Tutors—Kendel

Peer tutoring is really helpful to student learning because students know how other students think. They can sometimes explain things to other students in a way that is easier to understand. Peer tutors are also less intimidating. A student will be more likely to ask a question or share their thoughts because they are talking to a peer. One example of the benefits of peer tutoring was when I was tutored on my research paper outline. It really helped me to get all of my thoughts in order and to get things down on paper. I was having some real organizational problems, and my tutor let me use them as a sounding board. My tutor kept asking helpful questions on why I wanted to put something here or there, and why did that make sense. I felt that the session was really successful. I got all of my thoughts organized, and I was ready to start writing!

Having Someone to Show Them the Ropes—Stephany

Last year, as a junior, I had to transfer to a new school where I didn't know any of the students. To my dismay, we were assigned a research paper, and I had no idea what my paper would be about. I struggled with coming up with a topic and with doing the research. At my previous school, I had always fancied myself a pretty good writer, but as I heard my new teacher's long list of demands, I realized that I had never written a real research paper. I suddenly felt very unsure about my writing skills. Thankfully, my teacher thought I needed additional help, considering I was a new student, and sent me over to the writing center after class to set up an appointment. There, I would be taught how research papers were done at this high school.

Just as I began to hyperventilate internally, a tutor from the center came to offer their expertise. At first, I was reluctant, but I finally mustered up the courage to ask for help. I don't remember exactly what my question was, but I do remember that I ended up changing my topic. I no longer was going to write about something so dull. That quick chat with the tutor led me to determine a topic and begin the research. I noticed the improvements right away.

> So sometimes working with a peer can make the tutee more inclined to think about their improvements, rather than automatically doing them because their teacher told them to.

My first experience at the writing center was filled with enthusiasm, friendly smiles, and productivity. During this brief appointment, I really got to know my tutor and grew comfortable with talking about my ideas. I wouldn't have been as open with my plans if I were sharing them with the teacher who would be correcting my paper. In the writing center, I also got things started ahead of time. Procrastination is a big issue for me. I learned that I had to have things done ahead of time in order to get feedback and still have time to revise. For the first time, I wasn't up until two o'clock in the morning trying to finish my research paper (like many of my peers were). When I went for additional help along the way, I was always greeted warmly and left feeling better about my paper than when I came in. Sometimes just talking out something in a quiet environment can be the biggest help, and with each visit, I found that constant assurance from the tutor helped me know that I was on the right track.

Writing Centers Help Tutees Improve in All Subjects—Sarah

What students learn in the writing center can assist them in multiple classes. I remember my first time in the writing center, back in my freshman year. Asking for help was, and still is, definitely scary because it's a way of admitting your flaws. When I first walked in, I was nervous because I didn't want my tutor thinking I was stupid and didn't know how to write a paper. However, all of the flaws that were in my paper ultimately made me a stronger writer. If I made a mistake in my writing, the tutor simply pointed it out and explained it to me, which helped me not make that same mistake again. My writing ability grew immensely. The techniques I applied to my English papers could easily be used for my history and religion papers as well.

BENEFITS OF TUTORING TO THE TUTORS

Although writing centers are designed to benefit the tutees, writing centers that are staffed with trained peer tutors have additional benefits for the tutors themselves. As students who have been both tutees and tutors, we have seen our writing transformed not only by the help we have received but also by the guidance we have given to others. In this section, Emma shares how increased confidence in her own tutoring led her to tutor in unexpected places. Rachel reflects on becoming a part of a community of tutors. Jasmyne discusses how her own writing in a second language as well as tutoring English Language Learners (ELLs) taught her that approaches to writing transcend language. Kendel proves that tutoring is not one-sided by recalling how her tutee taught *her* a new strategy. Stephany, like many of us, speaks to how important it is to be patient and to recognize when a tutee has the same issue we ourselves struggle with. Sarah describes how she became a more analytical reader from working with students on their essays. Finally, Naba describes the types of sessions that keep students coming back to a tutor again and again.

Tutoring in Unexpected Places—Emma

The first moment I realized that the writing center had become a huge part of my life was while I was on the sidelines of a field hockey game. My team had just lost, and as the second half of the varsity game rolled around, my friend and I found ourselves pulling out homework. We reached into our composition folders to find the latest assignment, a "write about your writing process" paper, and before long we were tutoring each other. We took our papers apart piece by piece, following all the steps we'd been taught to use in a real session. This may seem like a weird thing to do while field hockey balls are being driven up and down the field beside you, but what's even weirder is how natural it felt.

Through tutoring, I have grown from a timid writer to a confident writing tutor. I take the title of tutor with me to every class, evaluating every genre of my own writing with more self-assurance and understanding than ever before. Freshman year, I couldn't imagine getting through a single tutoring session, and now I am a tutor in every aspect of my life.

A Community of Tutors—Rachel

When I was first exposed to the 20-minute conferences, tutoring logs, and observations, I was overwhelmed. Now, when I reflect on my work in the writing center, I fully appreciate the experiences working there has given me. I was never a group-savvy person until I discovered the benefits of having a community to share ideas, thoughts, and experiences with. I value all of the skills the writing center has developed in me and cherish the fact that the skills will be useful in college. I graduate in roughly a year and a half and cannot even begin to imagine the new heights this writing center will reach after I have gone. The program was new to me, I took a chance, I submitted my application, I received acceptance, I have learned, and I am thankful.

Tutoring Writing in Any Language—Jasmyne

Another dreaded essay. Even worse: I had to write it in Spanish. Once again, I was painfully reminded that being a tutor does not make me immune to common writing diseases. I am a firm believer in the saying, "Old habits die hard," so I was hesitant to discard the method to which I had grown so accustomed. Pour in the subject, stir in a verb, and sprinkle a few adjectives here and there—a time-honored recipe that guaranteed at least a "B." I began to write, but my beloved method failed me. Each word further added to the incoherency of the piece. Nothing was in its right place; nothing made sense. Just before all hope was lost, my tutoring flag went up. I came back to my senses and considered what steps I would take if I were writing the essay in English. After all, an essay is an essay whether in English or Spanish or Swahili. That is what is so beautiful about the writing process—it never changes. I referred back to my high school writing center's Seven Priorities of Writing: Appropriateness, Focus, Organization, Development, Surface Features,

Introduction/Conclusion, and Diction/Style. With the application of these valuable tools, I succeeded in creating a written masterpiece.

Not too long after my experience with the essay, I had the opportunity of tutoring an English Language Learner (ELL). I saw many of the same mistakes I had made when trying to write in another language. Fancy, ambiguous terms overshadowed the paper's purpose. I introduced him to the Seven Priorities process; we went step-by-step until only the bare bones of the paper remained. Leaving smaller issues like spelling and grammar aside, we worked on developing the paper's structure and organization. The goal was to make the piece understandable, and we did.

Tutors Learning from Their Tutees—Kendel

Peer tutoring is an essential part of learning for both tutor and student. Many think that only the tutee benefits from the exchange, but that is a misconception. In reality, the tutor actually learns from the tutee. For example, I had a research paper outline due for a class. I was helping a student with their paper and soon realized that they already completed a part of the assignment that I was currently struggling with: my thesis. I asked the student how they came up with such a fantastic thesis, and they said, "I got all of my thoughts down on paper and then condensed them into my thesis statement." I was amazed, and as I helped them with the rest of their paper, I realized that the tutee had indeed helped the tutor.

Patience and Procrastination—Stephany

Before becoming a peer tutor, my patience with teaching others was so thin. I could not even help my little sister with homework without throwing a tantrum when she began to daydream as I explained directions to her. But tutoring has taught me to be patient and to let people find their own answers.

As a tutor, I don't only help writers make a better paper, I help them become better writers. My peer tutor experience helped me get hired as a tutor for two boys: one in the fourth grade, the other in the sixth. With this job, I've noticed that I correct my tutees on mistakes I've made in my own past. An example is distraction: I have to really push my tutees to stay on task, but then I do the exact same thing when I'm at home doing my homework. I'll concentrate for the first 5 minutes, and then I find myself getting distracted by the rerun on television or answering a text message or an email that I received a while ago. This realization led me to quit cold turkey the bad habit of distraction. I now leave the television off while I do schoolwork and keep my phone as far away as possible. Overall, the tutoring experience has brought more benefits to me than to the tutees.

Tutors Becoming Analytical Readers—Sarah

Being a tutor has given me the ability to become a good reader. I now understand that a good paper is one the reader really wants to read. Recently, I was tutoring students on their history papers. All had the same topic, and their papers were all missing the same thing: analysis. Many students didn't know how to add analysis into their papers. I remembered key questions that could guide them when writing analysis: Why is it important? Why do I care? What effect did it have on the people/country? What effect does it have today? Without the analysis, their papers were a list of facts. After they added analysis, their papers were so much better and came to life. In the past, whenever my teacher would make a comment on my paper, saying I didn't have much analysis, I wouldn't understand why it was crucial. However, by being the tutor and reading weaker papers and stronger papers, I now fully understand what a good paper is. I am in no way a perfect writer, but by giving my tutees feedback, I am also giving myself feedback.

> **Tutors also become part of the student's writing process, which is a cool aspect of tutoring.**

Sharing and Celebrating the Tutees' Success—Naba

People who believe that tutoring is a boring job have clearly not tutored in a high school writing center. Tutors feel a true sense of accomplishment because they are able to help students every day and watch them grow as writers. Tutors also become part of the student's writing process, which is a cool aspect of tutoring. Part of a tutor's job is to get the words and ideas out of the tutee's head and onto their paper. As tutors listen to tutees read their papers, we become a part of their writing process because our presence and guidance helps the tutees turn good papers into great ones. I know that once a session is over, I am elated because the tutee is usually so thankful for my help and happy with their revised essay. This makes me happy. But the best part of tutoring is when I see a former tutee in the hallway who is proud they got an A on their essay, or when a tutee requests to work with me specifically, saying: "Hey, I'm the girl whose life you saved on that world history essay!"

Tutoring is fun and fulfilling. Take my most memorable session, for example. Alba came into the center panicked and stressed since her essay was due the next day. I calmed her down by telling her that we could extend our appointment to after school if we did not finish in time. After she read her essay aloud, I told Alba that she needed to add concluding sentences to connect her thesis to her individual paragraphs, which she then told me was exactly what her teacher had told her to do. I had her write down each argument and had her verbally explain each one until she was ready to form a proper concluding sentence. This method worked for each of her paragraphs. When our session ended, she just kept thanking me and telling me how relieved she felt. I was so happy that she really appreciated my help. But she did everything. I just guided her.

APPROACHES TO PEER TUTORING

We know you may be thinking, "Okay. So I have gotten a very clear picture of what peer tutoring is, but what is it all about? What can I, a teacher or administrator or even a high school student, expect to see happening in a tutoring session?" In the following section, peer tutors describe their own methods of tutoring. First, Allie describes her approach to tutoring with a simple six-step "recipe." Kendel then discusses her initial fears about tutoring, as well as how she worked with a reluctant tutee. Lastly, Nicole explains how her dyslexia does not define her but does make her a uniquely qualified tutor.

A Recipe for Being an Exceptional Tutor—Allie

When a peer tutor first starts out, they're nervous and excited. At least, that's how I felt when I first started tutoring this year! I thought a perfect way to explain the process would be to show how tutoring is like baking.

Step one: Start off the conference confidently and encouragingly. I always like to make sure my tutee is comfortable during our conference. I remember my freshman year I had to go to the writing center, and I was a bundle of nerves! I had butterflies in the pit of my stomach when I walked through the doors, signed in, and walked over to my tutor. I was probably nervous because it was my first session, and I had no idea what to expect. My tutor made me feel comfortable by offering their name and finding common ground between the two of us. A little tip? Make 'em laugh! In my opinion, it always lightens the mood. This part of the conference is the basis of your whole existence. For a cookie, at least, it's the flour that makes the cookie possible.

Step two: Ease your way into the conference. Ask your tutee what they are writing about, and if they have any concerns with their paper that they want to address. If you give them control over the conference, then it doesn't seem like you, the tutor, are monopolizing it. Giving the tutee control is like letting them stir the batter before separating the dough onto cookie sheets.

Step three: Manage expectations. At the writing center, we have 20- to 30-minute conferences, depending on whether the tutee arrives during their lunch or after school on Wednesdays. I like to give my tutee a heads-up about what will happen so they are aware of time restraints and what exactly will go on during the conference. I inform the tutee how long we have and that it is very possible we will not get through the entire paper. I also tell them that I will help them with their paper, not fix it or rewrite it for them. Managing the expectations of the tutee is as vital to the conference as measuring the amounts of water, oil, and other ingredients into your batter.

Step four: Ask the right questions. During conferences, I try my hardest to keep my tutee engaged in the conference. Sometimes editing or rewriting a paper can be tedious or even boring for students. You don't want to assume what the paper is about, so the more talking the tutee does, the better. I also like to keep the tutee engaged, so they have a good experience at the writing center and consider coming back. It's also a good way to share their ideas and get feedback. Observing another tutor's conference is a good way to try different techniques. Mix it up a bit! Throw in some cinnamon to your normally bland cake or extra chocolate chips to your brownies. Add some spice to your own special technique.

Step five: Listen to your tutee. Listening is the key ingredient to this recipe. Tailoring your tutoring skills to the student is a critical technique. By listening, you can get to know the tutee's writing style and their ideas as to how they want to write the paper. When they devise an idea, accept it, and work off it. If the idea doesn't fit with the curriculum, utilize constructive criticism. Say, "I like that idea, but maybe we could . . ." and add on to whatever you're working on to the end of that sentence. Listening to the tutee is like reading the instructions off the back of a brownie-mix box: You measure everything correctly, stir it all up, spread it in the pan, and set the oven to the right temperature. Just as you do not want to burn your brownies, you do not want to dissatisfy your tutee.

Step six: Fin! When the conference comes to an end, give your tutee a few last suggestions. Mine tend to end like this before I say good-bye: "Thank you so much for coming! I hope you come back. Remember when you go home to work on what we learned today. Do you have any other questions?"

Enjoy your baked goods! Delightful, aren't they?

Tutoring Anxiety and Working with Reluctant Tutees—Kendel

The high school writing center helps both the tutor and the tutee. The tutee receives help on assignments from their peers in a positive environment. The tutor also learns more about writing in the process. For example, I learned a lot in our tutor training class. I was really nervous about how I would act with a tutee and what I would say if the conversation stalled. I was nervous that I wouldn't be able to help them with all of their problems because I would not know the answer myself. It is my natural tendency to grab a paper to read and correct, but then the tutee doesn't learn as much. I really thought that the most important thing I learned was how the tutee was supposed to do all the work. It is like the expression: "Give a man a fish, and he will eat for a night, but teach him to fish, and he will eat for a lifetime."

Another example of how the writing center benefits both the tutor and the tutee is evident in how I really enjoyed my tutoring experience with one of the classes at our school. I thought that the students had lots of insightful ideas that helped me further my own knowledge in the subject. It felt really great to be able to help someone and to see their stress turn into relief. There was one student who just wanted me to fill out her skeleton outline sheet for them, and I gently pushed the paper back and said, "What do you think you should write?" The student looked frustrated at first, but then we talked about the pros and cons of both sides of the argument they were looking at, and we figured out which side they were on. Then I asked them to write down why they chose that side. The student eventually condensed those reasons into a beautiful thesis statement. I thought all of the students were generally very cooperative and that tutoring was a lot of fun!

Having Dyslexia Makes Me a Great Tutor—Nicole

I am currently in both honors and Advanced Placement classes. I am a peer tutor at my high school. I am also dyslexic. I know, you may be thinking, "How can someone with dyslexia be able to tutor? Why should and how can someone with learning disabilities be able to help others with or without learning challenges?" I have been asked these hurtful questions time and time again. If you will allow me to do so, I will let you in on a little secret. Are you ready?

Well, the secret is that students who have learning disabilities can actually, in some ways, make better peer tutors than students without learning disabilities! I know from my own personal experiences that I have faced a lot of challenges with learning. I have developed techniques and strategies that fit my learning style and better help me to complete my work. I have developed a color-coding system that I apply to everything from taking notes to formatting essays to reading. This color-coding system helps me stay organized and remember my material. I have had a lot of people criticize and tease me for this. (I said "people" in that last sentence because the teasing and criticizing that I have endured comes not only from my peers but also from teachers and adults.) Whenever someone teases me about my color-coding system, I tell them that countless tests have been conducted that conclude people, both with and without learning differences, remember things better if they highlight or write them in different colors other than yellow (for highlighting) or black (for writing). I have also developed a flashcard system that I use to take notes on important information and to learn vocabulary.

I feel that I am more qualified in some areas to be a peer tutor because I have a bank of countless strategies, techniques, and helpful tips to offer to students who may be having a hard time with schoolwork. If a student is having trouble taking notes, I can offer up my organizing system and color-coding system for notes. These systems can be customized to fit everyone's own needs, making the system more effective than general note-taking strategies. I recently taught a student my color-coding system in a tutoring session. The student had been really confused as to how to organize their research paper outline. They were also having trouble locating information once they put it in an outline. I customized my color-coding system for the student's needs for the paper and then explained it. I suggested that the main topic be highlighted in a dark, bold color, such as blue. The subtopics would then be highlighted in a light shade of blue. Finally, I suggested that the information written below each subtopic be written in a different shade of blue. The student grabbed a highlighter, blue pencil, and blue pen and got right to work. They said that my advice was extremely helpful and that they planned on transferring this method to other areas of their schoolwork.

I have also offered other techniques and strategies to peers and adults who are living and working in the real world. I taught my brother my notecard system. My brother was trying to get a job at Chili's. In order to become a waiter there, the applicant had to pass a test consisting of re-creating the entire menu from memory. My brother failed this test miserably, so he asked me to help him. I customized my notecard system to fit the information he needed to know to pass the test. After 2 nights of intense studying, my brother retook the test and passed it with flying colors. The techniques that I teach not only apply to school learning but also real-world experiences.

"Don't judge a book by its cover" applies to picking peer tutors. Don't misjudge a person because of their learning disabilities. People often refer to me as the smart dyslexic girl. Although I am dyslexic, I view myself as completely separate from my learning disability. I am not defined by my dyslexia. I am defined by the actions I take to learn from my learning disability in order to be a better person and peer tutor.

HOW PEER TUTORING CONTINUES TO SHAPE ME

Peer Tutoring Skills and the Creative Process—Jon-Carlos, Filmmaker

When you're put into the role of guiding someone in the process of writing, you're helping them shuffle and sift through their thoughts to create a defined and direct statement of will. Needless to say, organizing your thoughts is about as easy as looking for a light switch in a room with no walls while blindfolded. The journey of writing is literally that—a step into a thick darkness where you must learn to cast aside your normal senses and rely on the only tool left—instinct, intuition, your gut feeling, your Third Eye. Call it what you like, but the core of writing comes from this hidden sense, and the only way to reach it is through thinking your way there.

> **My writing center experiences gave me the tools and understanding to find bridges to people with whom I would never have worked so intimately otherwise.**

My personal experience with the idea of thinking through writing began as a writing coach during my senior year of high school. Immediately after that, I spent 4 years working at a university writing center while I worked on my Film Production B.A. I did some occasional work at that center for an additional year after my graduation. Since then, my life has been mostly dominated by filmmaking projects. While I am no longer immersed in the writing center world, I do know that by working there, I internalized the methodology of helping people think and write for the purpose of my work. In the same way that I would challenge a student to "kill their darlings" and question an argument, I do the same to sort through the obvious and discover the golden ideas buried beneath my own fears and defenses. No idea worth having comes easily; all you can do is prepare for the battle.

Once someone has gotten to the point of gathering their experiences and inspirations into an idea they can be passionate about, they have reached a heavy crux. Writing is often a journey in darkness, and with two people involved in the forming of something new, things can become even more complicated. In order to work through innately chaotic ideas and thoughts, one must systematically carve away at abstractions until they take on shape and meaning.

Thinking, forming ideas, and collaborative writing especially spring from a patient act of passivity—namely, observation. When I coached, or tutored, writing, the first thing I did after meeting the writer was engage in a process of questioning and observation. Before even reading their writing, I thought it more important to figure out where they were coming from and how they communicated. I wanted to explore their general demeanor, knowing the student was key to reading their work. I knew that most of the time, individuals didn't express their own ideas well without some sort of training or at least great sense of will and clarity; as a result, I tried to mirror the student's point of view in order to know how to motivate the appropriate changes.

I also knew that deconstruction was sometimes paramount to writing and forming ideas. To the student gathering ideas, I often told them they would not realize what's worth keeping until they're willing to "kill your darlings," as the saying goes. I helped them realize that the first draft exists solely to be tested, shredded, and rebuilt with contradicting ideas. I encouraged students to challenge their own assumptions and even write the piece from a different point of view. As long something existed on a page or in front of them, there was something to remold. I found the best way to encourage people to deconstruct their own work is to go Socratic—the more questions and possibilities someone considers, the better the chance that they will, by sheer process of volume, eventually see their complete idea in front of them. That idea may just be disparate pieces that need a unified whole. (At that point in the session, we'd still be in the darkness, but at least we'd have a torch to light our way.)

Over time, a well-nurtured thought takes on a life of its own. Once a thought manifests, it is written, and eventually its meaning spreads. As disparate and chaotic as humans are, an idea is a singular thread that unites us all. As long as we can think, we can survive; all of our hopes, dreams, and fears lie first in ideas, then the will of our words, and finally, the power of the moment in action.

Bringing Tutoring to Music Teaching—Justin, Musician

In high school, I always felt like an open-minded guy. I was proud to be friends with classmates of all skin colors and socioeconomic backgrounds and never fell into a clique, or at least not for long. During my senior year, my high school opened a writing center staffed by volunteers and seniors from the AP English class. Working as a writing coach, I became aware of the very real distance separating me from many of my fellow students. My writing center experiences, starting in high school and continuing through my undergrad studies, gave me the tools and understanding to find bridges to people with whom I would never have worked so intimately otherwise. The skills and knowledge I picked up as a coach prepared me for life after college.

For all its diversity, my hometown sometimes failed on the principle of economic egalitarianism. I was born into a middle-class household, and though my family never had a great excess of money, I was blessed with the greatest privilege of all, a solid educational foundation. The writing center had me bumping elbows with some of my peers who weren't so fortunate. Aside from the well-rounded, clever, and charismatic students I had befriended, there were also students who fell through the cracks—they had lived in broken homes or had untreated (or undiagnosed) learning disabilities. Some of them sought attention and acted out, clowning for the broader student community, and others tried to make as little an impression as they could and passed by in the hallway, unnoticed.

The students of the former group were always difficult when I worked with them in the writing center. These were often popular students I was friendly with and had crudely joked with in our shared classes or at lunch. They usually wanted me to simply write their papers for them, which I at first attributed to their social status or laziness. After telling them up front that I wouldn't cheat, I was faced with obstinate resistance. Many sessions wouldn't go anywhere, and all my persistence and prodding produced very little writing or even critical thinking in my peer. I knew these weren't stupid people, as I had firsthand witnessed the class clown's fiery wit and the football star's disciplined athleticism and strategy. With time, I came to understand their intransigence as a defense mechanism.

In college, I started coaching my freshman year and had a chance to see some of the tutees for my entire tenure. While coaching some of the regulars aroused in me the frustration of desperately trying to start a broken-down car, the intermittent successes were exhilarating. Witnessing the moment of enlightenment was like watching a fog clear before their eyes. I was proud of them.

When I landed a guitar-teaching position at a local performing arts studio, I brought with me the "coaching" philosophy. Rather than try to cram the music into the students' brain-holes, I tried to draw it out of them. This approach worked because the people and their situations were not very different. Just as students were introduced to the writing center through the compulsory education system (at least in high school), many of my guitar students were there because their parents bought them a loud instrument and demanded they take lessons. I had to deal with the same expectations—tutees would expect me to write papers, while guitar students just wanted to learn a song. Learning to coach guitar was a rocky road, but my experience as a writing coach helped me absorb some of the shock.

When I first started learning guitar, my teacher wrote out tablature, which is a form of notation detailing which fret of which string the guitarist should play. He taught me how to play songs, but I wasn't really learning that much about music. To a certain degree, this style of teaching is necessary so a guitar student can learn the fine-motor skills, but it's also missing higher-order concerns, such as ear training and understanding form, harmony, and other elements of music. Fortunately for coaches, these are all intuitive on a basic level. Much like language, most musical principles are intuitive and can be coached out of the tutee.

By employing the same techniques that I did coaching writing, my students were able to figure things out for themselves. The most gratifying thing was seeing the moment when everything clicked. Learning to coach writing in high school has transformed me into something of a coach in everything I do. In fact, I rarely ever think consciously about it. Having coached writing for roughly 6 years, it has become a natural extension of my personality, whether it's with a guitar student or just helping a friend or family who has come to me in need of help.

Shaping a Teaching Career—Hannah, English Teacher

I'm not sure exactly how I found out about the new writing center, but I do know that I was lured in with an honors elective credit, a vintage record player, and all the cheap coffee I could drink. I also believed that the invitation to be a tutor confirmed my superior skills as a writer and would allow me to frequently show off those talents. A senior in high school, I had known for several years that someday I would be an English teacher. This career goal was motivated partly by a desire to help others and share with them my love for language and literature, but also, less generously, a vision of endless opportunities to impress my future students with my knowledge and skills—as well as access to unchecked power.

One of my first tutoring sessions was with a fellow senior who was hesitant about her college application essay. I zeroed in on her weak vocabulary, peppering her with suggestions for replacements that I thought sounded intellectual but were probably stilted and pretentious. As our session progressed, her pen somehow migrated to my hand, and she spoke up less and less. I interpreted her silence as awe and continued my rampage through her essay. By the end of our session, the writing might have improved, but it was no longer hers. She left without so much as a thank-you, and I grumbled to myself about her ingratitude. My expertise could have made the difference between a thin letter and a fat one from her dream school!

She returned to the writing center a couple of weeks later, and though my schedule was wide open, she chose to work with another tutor and scrupulously avoided making eye contact with me. Watching other tutors at work, I realized most student-clients were drawn not to the tutors who were most skilled at writing, but to those who were the most mature listeners. They seemed to appreciate these tutors' sensitive feedback, thoughtful questions, and sincere encouragement. It seemed that the less the tutor said, the more comfortable the client felt taking responsibility for the direction of the session and the revision. Slowly, I adapted my own style to be more patient. This quietness left room for me to discover humbling weakness in my own "superior" writing, as well as my attitude.

Working as a writing tutor didn't spark my decision to become a teacher, but it fueled my resolve and profoundly affected my vision of the type of teacher I wanted—and still want—to be. Though I can still be ruthless with a red pen, I'm also careful to note where a student has succeeded. Truly dreadful writing merits a one-on-one revision session, rather than the mutual frustration of an

F. I still have much to learn about teaching writing effectively and compassionately, but I'm confident in the foundation that was laid by my tutor training.

Ten years after I attended the ribbon-cutting ceremony at my high school's new writing center, I again find myself in the thrilling position of helping to establish a secondary writing center. Reconnecting to this unique space has invigorated and inspired me. Training the tutors pushes me to take a hard look at my own practices as a writing teacher and renews my commitment to self-improvement. As a peer tutor, I regarded working in a writing center as a fun way to pass a class period or earn money, a reminder to seek feedback on my own writing, and a useful tool to develop skills for my future career. From my new perspective as an English teacher, I understand that writing centers offer so much more. They are catalysts of student collaboration, growth, and empowerment. They create independent writers who value process equally to product. They foster relationships between students who may have never met or spoken otherwise. They also ease the burden on teachers, making it possible for them to increase the breadth and depth of the writing they ask of their students, and provoking professional conversations about writing instruction. And sometimes, writing centers even offer free coffee.

FINAL THOUGHTS

When we, the high school tutors, started to work on this chapter, we were surprised to learn that most high schools don't have writing centers. We couldn't and still can't understand why. High school writing centers enable both tutees and tutors to transform themselves as students, as writers, and as people. Tutees are able to come as they are, insecurities and all, to a place where someone relatable is able and willing to listen to them, to really hear them, and to offer them guidance as they learn to write in different genres. Through learning how to work with their peers, tutors learn more about writing and more about their own strengths. The impact of peer tutoring in a high school writing center continues to reverberate in tutors' lives through college and into their careers. We think that there can be no more compelling arguments for the creation of high school writing centers than those voiced by current and former peer tutors.

CHAPTER SEVEN

Integrating Reading into the High School Writing Center

Jennifer Wells

Starting any new program at a high school is like building IKEA furniture without instructions. You have all these components, these parts, from models of other programs, from classes you've taken, from books and journals you've read, and from conversations you've had at conferences or in hallways. You may have an idea of what you think it should look like, but you're not sure how to assemble all these pieces into a whole. Or at least that's how it was for us when our high school's administration heeded the entreaties of the long-suffering English department Chair and agreed to fund a brand-new writing center. And that is definitely how it was for me when I was hired to run it.

At the time, I had just finished my M.A. in English Composition, and thus, was a member of the everything-in-my-studio-apartment-is-furnished-by-IKEA-and-has-unpronounceable-names-like-PLUKFPYORP club. I was also an aspiring IKEA hack, that is, someone who takes a prefabricated IKEA product and either switches out parts to make it more individualized, or someone who repurposes a piece to turn it into something entirely new. And so it came to be with our writing center. I looked at preexisting models of both college and high school writing centers and, eventually, of literacy coaching programs. Though I had a background in college composition and post-secondary reading, I delved into secondary content-area literacy theory and pedagogy. From this array of source material, my colleagues and I constructed, sometimes purposefully, sometimes by fortunate accident, a model of a high school writing center that works for us, and that may work for other schools as well.

THE MERCY READING AND WRITING CENTER: CREATING A COMMUNITY OF LITERACY

What makes this model somewhat unique is that we purposely and explicitly integrated reading into the writing center, the reasons for which I will explain below, and created a full-time faculty position that is a hybrid of a writing center director and a literacy coach. In the pages to follow, I will discuss the history and theory of content-area literacy, literacy coaching, and high school writing centers in order to explain how our center, by combining all three, mediates some of the limitations of each individual area of practice. Then, I will share how this works for us in real life, by describing both what occurs on a typical day in our center (inasmuch as any day is typical), and what additional things the center has done to foster a community of literacy in our school. Last, I will offer a realistic assessment of where we've succeeded and where we still need to grow, and in doing this, provide both ideas and cautions for those interested in creating reading and writing centers at their own high schools.

Though I direct the center, I am going to use the pronoun *we* to describe what we do, because the success of any program depends on the collaborative efforts of those both directly and indirectly involved in it. Additionally, while many essays on high school writing centers begin with some sort of history of how the center came to be, for the purposes of this one, I am going to skip past that. What is important to know is that there were several factors that shaped what the center would ultimately become—namely that our school had just switched to a block schedule, and so our students went from having free periods to being in class, or an assigned study hall, all day. This meant that, though we had a room for the writing center, we would have vast periods of the day where a very limited number of students would be free to access it. So, we needed to figure out ways to take the writing center on the road. Second, we were also experiencing what is commonly known as the adolescent literacy crisis.

THE LITERACY CRISIS WEARS ABERCROMBIE AND FITCH

More often than not, when people hear about the literacy crisis, they assume it describes a situation that only exists in underfunded, underperforming, urban public schools. Additionally, some educators succumb to the Myth of the Perfect Past and believe in a magical time when students were, if not perfect, then close to it, and that today's students are irreparably flawed. Both kinds of thinking distract from the true complexities of the current literacy crisis, which is not endemic to a certain type of school system, nor is it inhibited by socioeconomic barriers. Additionally, it may not be that our students are better or worse than their counterparts 20 years ago, but that they live in a world that requires multiple literacies. The International Reading Association explains, "High school graduates are required to interpret a wide range of reference materials: journal articles, memoranda and other documents that may contain technical information, including intricate charts and graphs. Increasingly, they are expected to judge the credibility of courses, evaluate arguments, develop and defend their own conclusions, and convey complex information in ways that will either advance scholarship in a discipline or contribute to workplace productivity" (2006, p. 1). Therefore, whether our adolescents enter the workforce directly or enter college largely unprepared (Alliance for Excellent Education, 2007), they are graduating without the critical literacy skills in reading and writing that they will need to navigate their futures.

So, we should not have been surprised when the literacy crisis showed up on the front doorstep of our small, parochial, all-girls high school. Located between wealthy Bay Area suburbs to the west and a working-class suburb to the east, our school, embracing the many worlds our students come from, serves a socioeconomically, ethnically, and religiously diverse population. Yet, as a private school, we are exempt from the external pressures and the constantly shifting yardsticks supplied by state-mandated standardized tests. There are numerous benefits to this, but at the same time, we have limited access to the types of data (valid or not) that might have confirmed what we ultimately suspected: Our students' overall reading and writing abilities had slowly declined over the decades that many of us had been teaching here.

So, before we opened our center for business, we tried to find out exactly what was going on with our students' reading abilities, at least from the teachers' perspectives. We distributed an open-ended survey to the faculty to find out more about the types of writing and reading students were doing in their classes and what the faculty's specific concerns were about their students' reading and writing abilities.

From the responses, we found that the most frequently cited areas of concern were "reading comprehension," "distinguishing main ideas from supporting details," and the "inability to make inferences." In addition, but to a lesser degree, the faculty was also worried about the students' "reading rates" and "reading discipline." A smaller number of faculty members were frustrated with their students' "vocabulary."

The responses from the survey clearly indicated that the faculty felt that the students needed serious development in reading. In short, we had a problem. And we weren't alone. The National Assessment of Educational Progress' (NAEP) long-term trend reading assessment measures students' abilities to "locate specific information, make inferences based on information in two or more parts of a passage, and identify the main idea in a passage" (Perie, Moran, & Lutkus, 2005, p. 1). The percentages of students who are able to do this have declined steadily since the test started being given in 1971. Clearly, there was a parallel between what the NAEP found students struggling with and the areas of concerns reported by the teachers at our school.

INTEGRATING READING INTO
THE WRITING CENTER AND HITTING THE ROAD

With the data from the faculty responses in mind, and with the knowledge that if we couldn't find a way to bring the writing center from its physical space to the rest of the campus then the center would be doomed to die a quick death, we decided to promote the new center to the faculty as a resource that would come to them, as well as one the students could go to. Specifically, we offered to work with interested faculty in designing and developing their own reading and/or writing activities in their various subject areas, and we also offered to come in and do "mini-workshops" with the students on everything from previewing a textbook to note-taking to using reader response journals to organizing information into an outline, and more.

Within weeks of offering the workshops, the times on our calendar not already blocked off for students were quickly filled with in-class workshops. Approximately 30% of our faculty invited us to come into their classrooms, which, while not an overwhelming majority, was more than we had hoped for. After the first month of doing in-class workshops, the teacher feedback was positive, and through word of mouth, several additional teachers contacted us to work with them. By the end of our first month, we had seen 90% of our entire student population, whether through an in-class workshop, a workshop or consultation in the writing center, or an online consultation (via email). In this way, we were able to make the new reading and writing center immediately useful to both faculty and students, and looking back, this was the best possible move we could have made to ensure our long-term success.

Three months after we had begun offering the workshops, we discovered that what we had been doing was extremely similar to an idea that, at that time, was just gaining momentum in literacy education circles: literacy coaching. All of a sudden, what we had been doing not only had a name but also had a small but growing community of practitioners, research, and literature. So, while we stumbled upon literacy coaching as a way to address faculty concerns with reading and as a way to create a center that would be sustainable on our restrictive schedule, it was a fortuitous and timely accident. Inasmuch as practice often precedes theory in secondary education (in spite of what we might want otherwise), when we discovered that we weren't alone, we immediately began to see how literacy coaching and writing center theory and pedagogy, which both have roots in and/or relationships with the Writing Across the Curriculum movement, attempt to respond to similar issues, albeit with different foci.

LITERACY COACHING:
WHERE HAVE YOU BEEN ALL MY LIFE?

That we had not heard of literacy coaching makes sense, since, depending on how you look at it, it is either new wine or old wine in a new wineskin. We had heard of a time when schools had reading specialists, specialized teachers who either pulled groups of students out of their regular classes or taught their own basic reading classes. The English department chair who had been the driving force in persuading our administration to fund the new reading and writing center had begun her teaching career in 1974 teaching high school reading. The existence of these positions in the 1970s and early 1980s was the direct result of the 1965 Elementary and Secondary Education Act (ESEA), which authorized federal funds for low-income school districts to hire reading specialists. These specialists, or Title I teachers, worked specifically with developing readers (Dole, 2004). By the 1980s, many middle and high schools had been able to use federal funds to employ certified reading specialists to help "at risk" students, whether they were low-income or not, but at the end of that decade, when funding began to dwindle, reading specialists and reading programs took the hit (Sturtevant, 2003), along with other perceived auxiliaries such as music, art, and some afterschool sports programs. When I was in high school in the early 1990s, no one I knew had taken a reading class or had specialized reading instruction since grade school.

Then, in 2002, ESEA was reauthorized as No Child Left Behind, and Title I funding was included as a part of the reauthorization. However, instead of using the funding to enable specialists to work with small groups of students outside the classroom, the focus was on using the federal money to improve the quality of teaching in the "first," or primary, classrooms (Dole, 2004).

Teaching teachers across the content areas to include reading and writing strategies in their courses has been notoriously challenging, though not for a lack of interest. Content-area literacy, sometimes called LALAC (Language and Literacy Across the Content Areas) or, more often at the college level, WAC (Writing Across the Curriculum), has been the subject of study and discussion since the early 20th century. In the 1970s, the cognitive revolution in psychology laid the foundation for a resurgence of interest in reading instruction, and the publication of Harold L. Herber's methods text *Teaching Reading in Content Areas* (Moore, Readence, & Rickelman, 1983). Since then, many teacher education programs have required that their pre-service teachers take a course in either reading or content-area literacy. However, having pre-service teachers take one course a year or more before entering the classroom cannot insure long-term success. In-service or professional development has been another popular model for teaching faculty to integrate reading and writing into their courses. Yet, as anyone who has sat through one too many in-services can attest, these infrequent and often seemingly random trainings don't usually translate into major curricular change (O'Brien, Stewart, & Moje, 1995; Sturtevant, 1996).

So it was the confluence of these two streams—the funding shift to increasing teacher quality and the realization that teacher preparation courses and sporadic in-services don't result in sustained professional development—that created the river of momentum that enabled the reading specialist role of the 1970s and 1980s to evolve into that of reading coach or "literacy coach," someone who would work alongside faculty to help them become better teachers of reading in their content-area courses.

> **Since the coach is immersed in the local context and culture of the school they serve, they are in a better position than some outside agent to help advise the school when literacy-related plans are made.**

Though the emergence of literacy coaching has a complicated relationship with the much-maligned NCLB, without the emphasis on qualified teachers, the need for reading coaches or literacy coaches would not have been as urgent. Since 2004, at least 7,000 schools have hired literacy coaches, though many of those coaches work on the elementary level, and many of those coaches were brought in alongside prepackaged programs like the dubious Reading First program (Niedzwiecki, 2007). In the annual "What's Hot: What's Not" column in *Reading Today*, literacy coaching has made the "hot" list numerous times.

Although it is not known exactly how many literacy coaches are working at the secondary level, the number is far less than the number working at the elementary level. However, with adolescent literacy becoming a more prominent issue, both in the media and within education circles, it is likely that over the next decade, educators will have to look more closely at how they can more fully integrate reading instruction across the content areas.

WHAT DOES A LITERACY COACH DO?

One of the defining characteristics of literacy coaches is that they are often required to be experts in many areas. Essentially, literacy coaches work with faculty on an ongoing basis to help them find ways to teach students the literacy skills and strategies necessary for academic, and life, success. Although they may occasionally work directly with students, their "major role is to work with content teachers across the curriculum" (Sturtevant, 2003). They may team teach, but more often, they observe and support classroom teachers and spend time working with the teacher preplanning new strategies and debriefing afterward. In order to be successful, the literacy coaches need to have a variety of skills. They must be able to articulate the purpose of their literacy program to teachers, and they must understand relevant theories in the areas of literacy learning, adult learning, leadership, and professional development. They need to be adept at working with a range of faculty, not all of whom will be happy to see them. They should also be able to collect and analyze data, communicate with and help guide administrators through literacy-related decisions, and engage in their own continued professional growth as literacy educators (Fisher, 2007).

Ideally, a literacy coach serves only one school and is able to collaborate with teachers of all levels and content areas. Effective coaching is "ongoing, job-embedded professional learning," and thus it is crucial that the coach be given ample opportunities to work with faculty over a sustained period of time (Shanklin, 2006). Since the coach is immersed in the local context and culture of the school they serve, they are in a better position than some outside agent to help advise the school when literacy-related plans are made. When literacy coaching is effective, teachers and coaches work collaboratively, and since teachers are supported on an ongoing basis, they are more likely to step outside their normal comfort zones and try new things.

THE SHORTFALLS OF LITERACY COACHING AND HIGH SCHOOL WRITING CENTERS

The history of high school writing centers is more difficult to write than the history of literacy coaching because while high school centers are not new in the way literacy coaching programs might be conceived to be, far, far less has been written about them. Also, though there is undoubtedly a relationship between the evolution of high school writing centers and their college-level counterparts, almost all of the literature about writing center history is devoted to parsing the long and complex history of the college writing center (Boquet, 1999).

What we do know about early high school writing centers stems mostly from Pamela B. Farrell's seminal text *The High School Writing Center: Establishing One and Maintaining One* (1989). What is important to note is that two of the earliest centers—Farrell's, which began in 1981, and William Speiser's, which began in 1970—were both born out of an interest in fostering writing across the curriculum at their respective high schools.

High school writing centers naturally support writing across the curriculum goals in that writing centers can help make students' thinking on any subject more transparent (Nicolini, 2006). Writing centers can open up dialogue between faculty on how writing can be taught, and can help students see writing in a new way, a way of learning and communicating in all their classes. High school teachers' schedules are usually so full that they have little time to conference with students individually about their writing, and so writing centers make it possible for teachers in all subject areas to enable their students to get personalized feedback that teachers might not realistically have time to give (Bottoms et al., 1987).

For all the wonderful and necessary work writing centers do for writing across the curriculum and by working individually with students, it seems that many are not meeting the need for *content-area literacy*—that is, writing *and* reading across the curriculum. At the same time, literacy coaches, for all the wonderful and necessary work they do with faculty and the teaching of reading, rarely work directly with students or with the faculty on teaching writing. Yet, both high school writing centers and literacy coaching are a response to the same need: to give students the reading *and* writing skills they need to succeed in any subject. Therefore, one of the most compelling arguments for integrating reading into the writing center on the student level, and for integrating literacy coaching into the writing center's work on the faculty level, is that it confronts the need for improved content-area literacy in a way that is simultaneously top-down and bottom-up.

A DAY IN THE LIFE OF
THE MERCY READING/WRITING CENTER

Secondary education is full of intellectual arguments that sound wonderful on paper but are difficult to turn into real practice. How can a writing center support reading? How can a writing center director also be a literacy coach? What does a day in the life of a center that embraces both reading and writing look like?

Just as no two high schools are exactly alike, no two high school reading/writing centers are, nor should be, the same. What follows is a brief description of the things that might occur on any given day in our reading/writing center. Following that is a brief description of activities and workshops that have helped us to move toward creating a community of literacy at our school, with the reading/writing center as its home base.

8 a.m. Religion IV: Inner Journey

Lead a workshop to introduce senior students to *Letters to a Young Poet* by Rainer Maria Rilke. Students bring a printout of one of his poems, then cut each word out, so they end up with a hundred or more individual words. Students then rearrange words to create their own "Found Poem" (Dunning & Stafford, 1992). They paste their poems into their writing journals. Afterward, the teacher and I co-facilitate a discussion on the various themes that came up in the students' poems (loss, sadness, despair, hope), most of which are also Rilke's themes in *Letters*. The found poems become an inductive opener, an introduction to Rilke and his poems and, most important for their upcoming reading, an introduction to his themes.

9:20 a.m. Advisory (Homeroom)

Students drop in to make appointments for later in the day or week or to follow up on a previous conference.

10:00 a.m. World History

The first of an ongoing series of mini-workshops to help guide sophomore students through writing their first high school research paper takes place. To get them to see research writing as argument, we get them to talk about what happens in a courtroom trial. There is a judge and sometimes jurors, attorneys, witnesses, and evidence. We talk about opening and closing arguments, about presenting evidence, about convincing the jury. Then we draw parallels between the function of an opening statement and the function of an introductory paragraph, including the function of an introductory paragraph.

10:45 a.m. AP U.S. History

We hold a mini-workshop on annotation (Porter-O'Donnell, 2004). The juniors are struggling with the APUSH textbook, as it is the first college-level, nonfiction text many of them have encountered. Although this is a class of generally mature readers, the strategies that have led them to success with reading thus far are starting to break down. They can't read it once and glean all the information. They are having trouble knowing which facts are important. Teaching them to "talk back to the text" allows them to read more actively, and through their dialogue, they notice which details are more central and which are supporting. They practice annotating two pages and are very surprised to discover that the textbook author has a sarcastic sense of humor.

11:20 a.m. Student Lunch Group A

Individual student conferences are held. Melissa brings in her college application essays; we've met six times this semester already, and she, in a mix of frustration and pride, admits she's never written so many drafts of any one essay in her life. Jamila brings her ninth-grade biology textbook and says she spends an hour a night reading for biology, and she doesn't know what she's supposed to take notes on. Together, we discuss how she might "preview" some of the textual features of the biology book before she begins reading a section (e.g., look at headings and subheadings, section objectives, chapter summaries, photos/graphics) in order to "predict" what the reading will be about. She practices on one section. Afterward, we review the section using the same strategies. For her notes, we use the section objectives (e.g., "Explain the structure of cells") to guide her responses.

12:10 p.m. Lunch (between student lunch periods)

12:50 p.m. Student Lunch Group B

Individual student conferences are held.

1:40 p.m. Teachers Do Their Own Work in the Center

We get into an informal conversation on thesis statements and how difficult it is to get students to learn what they are and how to write them. We brainstorm some different strategies, and I share two excerpts from books I have on the center's shelf (*Everything's an Argument*; *They Say, I Say*). Two teachers decide they are going to try an activity based upon our discussion.

3:00 p.m. Individual Student Appointments

Abby, a sophomore in Honors English, brings a creative nonfiction assignment based on *A Tale of Two Cities*. She has to tell her own "Tale of Two" and can write it from the perspective of any two things she chooses to write about. A strong analysis essay writer, Abby is "freaked out" by creative writing and also overwhelmed by how much choice she has in this assignment. We start by talking about her ideas until she finds one she's excited about, and then we make notecards with quick sketches of possible moments in her story. We then discuss different ways of structuring narration (begin with a flashback, begin at the end, begin at the beginning) and play around with structure by reorganizing the notecards. After Abby leaves, Sasha, a junior, drops in with a poem by e.e. cummings, an essay by Thoreau, and a writing prompt that asks her to compare the rhetorical devices used in each. "I don't get either of these," she sighs, and so we begin by first revisiting the idea of rhetoric: that writers use tools to convey a tone or stance and that they do this for a purpose. I explain that her job as the reader is to first identify which words or lines she responds to and then try to figure out why the author might want the reader to have that response. We spend the next 45 minutes going through the poem and essay, line by line. By the end, she has identified literary devices and has a thesis about the authors' intended effects on the reader.

CREATING A COMMUNITY OF LITERACY

In addition to the everyday happenings in the reading/writing center, we host a number of clubs and other activities for students, faculty, and parents that further our goal of creating a schoolwide community of literacy. As part of the broader scope of the reading and writing center, we wanted to make ourselves useful to all the members of our school community and also provide a center for a number of previously orphaned clubs and publications that were reading/writing-related. The reasons for this were both practical and political. Practically, by offering events and resources for the whole school community, we were able to reinforce our first message, which was that reading and writing involves everyone, and everyone can benefit from using the center. Politically, the more people the writing center has on their team, the better.

Literacy Activities for Students

In the fall, we run a series of workshops for seniors on writing college admissions essays. The reading/writing center also hosts the student book club, which is enormously popular, even with students who self-identify as being poor readers. Once a month, the students in the club select a book, they all read it on their own, and then they meet to talk about the book (and inevitably other things). Students in the *Mercy Excellence* Club design and edit the school literary arts magazine, *Mercy Excellence*, which features the best student writing, both academic and creative, along with the best student artwork. The Peer Reading and Writing Coaches Program recruits and teaches volunteer peer tutors how to work with students on both reading and writing in the center.

Literacy Activities for Faculty

In addition to offering in-class workshops, we also periodically put together optional, informal workshops to help faculty discover answers to questions such as "How can I get students to know more vocabulary?" or "Why don't students use the comments I write on their papers?" Also, once a year, the monthly faculty book club, which has been going strong for 10 years, joins with the student book club, and both faculty and students discuss a book together. This is the highlight of the book club for the student members because it is one of the first times they get to experience their teachers as equals. As student-centered as classroom teachers may try to be, students often feel there is only one way to discuss literature assigned in class. When they are in the book club, any and all interpretations are game, and when they can share those with their teachers, the playing field is leveled.

Literacy Activities for Parents

In talking with parents at various events, we discovered that many of them wanted to help their students become better readers, but they didn't know how. We also know from our observations and students' reports that often when parents try to "help" their children write, the parents take over, and the words and ideas become less the students' and more the parents'. So, now we offer "parents' nights" when we focus on teaching parents how they can best help their students. This not only gets parents to visit the reading/writing center, but it enables them to become partners in their students' education in ways they might not have known about before. Lastly, but crucially, by making the center useful to parents, the parents become allies of the center itself. Simply put, when the parents are happy, the administration is happy, so then we are happy.

REFLECTIONS ON THE
READING/WRITING CENTER MODEL

Every semester, we collect faculty evaluations, which have provided a wealth of useful feedback. To begin, the faculty who have used the reading and writing center the most, whether to refer their students to us or invite us into their classrooms, have reported an overall increase in their students' critical reading and writing abilities. Many faculty have been very receptive to the idea of having us in their classrooms because, as one teacher wrote, "Students get tired of hearing my voice. Sometimes they need to hear the same thing from a new voice to really hear it." One teacher reported that in her 40 years of teaching, she has made the most changes to the way she teaches writing in the past 2 years. She said, "The Reading and Writing Center has influenced me to be a better teacher in writing skills. When I am planning my day-to-day things, I've used the techniques you've taught in my classroom." Another teacher wrote that on her student evaluation forms, several mentioned that annotating had really helped them "understand the material, rather than just copying their notes out of the book." The faculty has also noticed a change in the students who visit the Reading and Writing Center. One faculty member explained, "When students are working together to solve something like how to write a good thesis statement, then the students are working together to use each other as resources." The 40-year veteran teacher also noted, "My research papers have been better than ever."

In spite of the positive feedback and unanimous support of the faculty who use the center, we of course have a number of faculty members who don't use the center. As Richard Kent (2006) explains, "It is a fundamental truth that creating and maintaining a writing center is a political act. The presence of a writing center changes the landscape of a school and creates a paradigm shift" (p. 29). This, then, might be perceived as a drawback of not having a formal literacy coaching program. Since teachers can opt to have us work with them and their students, or not, it is a much more informal process. Perhaps unsurprisingly, the English department, though supportive, infrequently utilizes the resources available. The social studies department and the religion department are our biggest faculty "clients," followed by arts (photography, yearbook, film). The students who most frequently use the center come for help on research papers, followed by college application essays, literary analysis essays, and reading nonfiction textbooks. So, although we have been able to augment the literacy development of all of our students in some of their classes, we still have a way to go.

> **If the writing center is using peer tutors, then those peer tutors should get training in not only conference with students about their writing but about their reading, as well.**

While we are extremely fortunate to be able to fund the full-time, faculty literacy coach/writing center director, many schools may not have that option. However, the need for integrating reading into the writing center is so great that there are a number of viable alternatives that should be explored. The first is that if the writing center is using peer tutors, then those peer tutors should get training in not only conference with students about their writing but about their reading, as well. At the college level, writing center tutors have reported feeling that their tutees are not adept at critical reading, and they felt it was important to help their tutees become better readers, but they had no idea how to do that (Griswold, 2006). Therefore, any writing center, whether at the secondary or college level, can be strengthened if their staff is trained in supporting reading. Another option is for the writing center director/supervisor to hold optional brown bag lunch sessions on integrating content literacy. Janet Allen's *Tools for Teaching Content Literacy* (2004) is an extremely approachable, practical, yet theoretically grounded book that our teachers have found invaluable. Since teachers aren't forced to attend the brown bag lunch, and since the meetings can be ongoing, it is an improvement over the mandatory in-service. Additionally, college writing centers are often interested in ways they can support their local high school community (Tinker, 2006), and so reaching out to them for help may be beneficial. Other alternatives might include a faculty listserv discussion, faculty/student book clubs, faculty pair-and-share where faculty share strategies that are working in their own classrooms, and so on.

FINAL THOUGHTS

At the end of our fourth year, the Mercy Reading and Writing Center achieved a 90% usage rate—that is, for the 2009–2010 school year, 90% of the student body visited the center, on their own, at least once. While this model of an integrated reading and writing center has worked well for us, it may not be the most practical answer for everyone. Yet, for those who are interested, there is a strong case to be made for funding a center that meets the needs of student readers and writers. Whether or not the reading and writing center has a literacy coach, student tutors, or community volunteers, there is no reason why those who work with students and/or faculty can't learn more about helping students of all abilities becomes more mature readers. Whether the literacy crisis wears Prada, Abercrombie and Fitch, or Roca; whether it arrives to school in a luxury SUV, by bus, or by foot; whether its first language is English or not, it is here at our door. Unless we keep looking for ways to build upon what we already know is successful, unless we try to integrate programs or combine resources or expand our conceptions of what our programs and services can do, unless we work with both students and faculty in order to meet somewhere in the middle, we will have let the crisis overtake us, and we will have let those who deserve better down.

REFERENCES

Allen, J. (2004). *Tools for teaching content literacy.* Portland, ME: Stenhouse.

Alliance for Excellent Education. (2007). *High school teaching for the twenty-first century: Preparing students for college.* Washington, DC: Author.

Boquet, E. H. (1999). "Our little secret": A history of writing centers, pre- to post-open admissions. *College Composition and Communication, 50*(3), 463–482.

Bottoms, L., Carter, J., McQuade, F., Upton, J., Lockward, D., Brinkely, E., Carroll, S., Mendenhall, C., & LGH. (1987). Round table: Is there a need for writing centers in secondary schools? If so what services should they provide? *English Journal, 76*(7), 68–70.

Dole, J. (2004). The changing role of the reading specialist in school reform. *The Reading Teacher, 57*(5), 462–471.

Dunning, S., & Stafford, W. (1992). *Getting the knack: 20 poetry writing exercises.* Urbana, IL: National Council of Teachers of English.

Farrell, P. B. (1989). A high school writing lab/center. In P. B. Farrell (Ed.), *The high school writing center: Establishing one and maintaining one* (pp. 9–22). Urbana, IL: National Council of Teachers of English.

Fisher, D. (2007). *Coaching considerations: FAQs useful in the development of literacy coaching.* Retrieved from http://www.literacycoachingonline.org/briefs/CoachingConsiderationsFinal020707.pdf

Graff, F. and Birkenstein, C. (2006). *They say, I say.* New York, NY: W.W. Norton.

Griswold, G. (2006). Postsecondary reading: What writing center tutors need to know. *Journal of College Reading and Learning, 37*(1), 61–72.

International Reading Association. (2006). *Standards for middle and high school literacy coaches.* Newark, DE: Author.

Lunsford, A.,& Ruszkiewicz, J. (1999). *Everything's an argument.* Boston, MA: Bedford St. Martins.

Kent, R. (2006). *A guide to creating student-staffed writing centers, grades 6–12.* New York: Peter Lang.

Moore, D. W., Readence, J. E., & Rickelman, R. J. (1983). An historical exploration of content area reading instruction. *Reading Research Quarterly, 18*(4), 419–438.

Nicolini, M. B. (2006). Making thinking visible: Writing in the center. *The Clearing House: A Journal of Educational Strategies, Issues and Ideas, 80*(2), 66–69.

Niedzwiecki, A. (2007). Organizational barriers to effective literacy coaching. *Journal of Language and Literacy Education 3*(1), 59–64. Retrieved from http://www.coe.uga.edu/jolle/2007_1/organizational.pdf

O'Brien, D. G., Stewart, R. A., & Moje, E. B. (1995). Why content literacy is difficult to infuse into the secondary school: Complexities of curriculum, pedagogy and school culture. *Reading Research Quarterly, 30*(3), 442–463.

Perie, M., Moran, R., & Lutkus, A. D. (2005). *NAEP 2004 trends in academic progress: Three decades of student performance in reading and mathematics* (NCES 2005–464). Washington, DC: U.S. Department of Education, Institute of Education Sciences, National Center for Education Statistics.

Porter-O'Donnell, C. (2004). Beyond the yellow highlighter: Teaching annotation skills to improve reading comprehension. *English Journal, 93*(5), 82–89.

Shanklin, N. L. (2006). What are the characteristics of effective literacy coaching? Retrieved from http://www.literacycoachingonline.org/briefs/CharofLiteracyCoachingNLS09-27-07.pdf

Sturtevant, E. G. (1996). Lifetime influences on the literacy-related instructional beliefs of experiences high school history teachers. *Journal of Literacy Research, 28*(2), 227–257.

Sturtevant, E. G. (2003). *The literacy coach: A key to improving teaching and learning in secondary schools.* Washington, DC: Alliance for Excellent Education.

Tinker, J. (2006). Generating cultures of writing: Collaborations between the Stanford writing center and high school writing centers. *The Clearing House: A Journal of Educational Strategies, Issues and Ideas, 80*(2), 89–91.

CHAPTER EIGHT

Connecting Pre-Service Teachers with High School Writers

Jill Adams

As a professor of English education, I often heard complaints about our English education pre-service teachers' lack of field experiences, and I saw the need to foster those interactions for pre-service teachers while working with secondary students on writing. It seemed essential to be present with them during these experiences in order to help them navigate some of the challenges they would face. Thus, an idea was hatched to create a secondary writing center based on service-learning principles.

Developing real-world skills is certainly something all teacher-educators strive to do with their pre-service teachers. This is clearly not as easy as it seems. English language arts pre-service teachers go into various classrooms for field experiences that may or may not demonstrate or connect with what is being taught in the college methods courses. Sometimes, the pre-service teachers have wonderful experiences because they have active participation in the classroom and participate in true, engaging, and reflective dialogue about their experiences. Other times, this does not occur for a myriad of reasons, including but not limited to pre-service teachers' lack of confidence, ineffective communication between the pre-service teacher and the cooperating teacher, and unclear expectations from college faculty.

Because collegiate faculty typically have limited involvement with the pre-service teacher's field experience beyond arranging the school placement, faculty are not usually available when challenges arise during the day. Although pre-service teachers can learn from all types of teaching situations, it is imperative that they also have strong mentors in the field who help them foster positive interactions with students.

Creating a secondary writing center where the director is a college faculty member or teacher-educator would enable our pre-service teachers to have a strong mentor on hand and give them the opportunity to practice what is being taught in their college classes. This would allow pre-service teachers to put the ideas presented in their coursework into action. The concept is simple: to create a secondary writing center that connects collegiate and secondary writers. The center's aim is to support all writers in all disciplines, to help make the most of pre-service teacher placement in the field by enabling them to participate in transformative experiences for secondary writers, and to make powerful connections between content in methods courses and the actual realities of the classroom. Instead of simply telling pre-service teachers how to coach student-writers, we wanted to offer these future teachers hands-on experience. Their college professor would remain nearby, modeling coaching techniques and providing support to the teachers as they work with students. The center would support the pre-service teachers, the secondary student-writers, and literacy instruction throughout the school.

INTEGRATING SERVICE LEARNING INTO THE WRITING CENTER

Goals for the writing center, as outlined by Childers, Fels, and Jordan (2004) in their article "The Secondary School Writing Center: A Place to Build Confident, Competent Writers," were quickly set:

> Work with all students, regardless of their innate talent, to build their confidence and competency as writers. Whether we are talking about students who need to fine-tune excellent papers or students who need to discover what they really want to say, a writing center can be a safe harbor within the sometimes stormy seas of the school day. (para. 1)

Our college's English education faculty and students worked to create a center that would embody this aim.

In creating this vision for our center's operation, we strove to incorporate the principle aspects of *service learning* into the center's activities. Although there are various interpretations of service learning, Learn and Serve America's National Service-Learning Clearinghouse website offers a definition with which many would agree:

> Service-learning is a teaching and learning strategy that integrates meaningful community service with instruction and reflection to enrich the learning experience, teach civic responsibility, and strengthen communities. ("What is service-learning?," n.d., para. 1)

Service-learning seemed to be the perfect fit for what we were trying to accomplish: to create a space for connecting collegiate and secondary writers. In turn, the experience would benefit both the pre-service teachers and the high school students. In an effort to achieve this aim, however, writing centers are often organized to "respond to the needs of an academic institution which sponsors it, the needs of (its) students, the needs of an instructor, or the needs of a course. The needs of the agency and the community often come last" (Eby, 1998, p. 7). Noting this challenge, we strove to fight against it and find a way to unite writers that would always clearly benefit both the secondary and collegiate students for a sustainable amount of time.

Implementing service-learning in the collegiate curriculum requires a lot of preparation. Janet Eyler and Dwight E. Giles Jr. (1999) investigated the steps to consider in their book *Where's the Learning in Service-Learning?* They discovered that the quality of the student's placement anchors the learning in the community experience and affects personal and interpersonal development. Eyler and Giles also noted that the application (described as the degree to which students can link what they are doing in the classroom to the community experience) can enhance the course objectives. Reflection is important as well, for it allows the students to step back thoughtfully to consider personal and interpersonal growth.

Giving students appropriate placements in the community is also imperative. In order to create high-quality placements, Eyler and Giles recommend that students do meaningful work, have important responsibilities and varied tasks, work directly with community partners, and receive support and feedback from agency staff. They also encourage the service to continue over a sustained period of time (pp. 190–191). Some scholars and educators believe that the service-learning movement has been fueled by an "uneasy sense that the academy is becoming increasingly irrelevant to the real issues of society" and that service-learning is a way to connect academia to the real world (Eby, 1998, p. 3).

With these key service-learning ideals in mind, we moved forward in creating our vision for our writing center. There was no budget, we didn't have a space, and college classes aren't generally held on high school campuses. But there was a need. In the collegiate arena, there seemed to be a lack of connection between what was taught in our Teaching Composition 7–12 class and the real-world application of the ideas we discussed—and encouraged—in class. For example, it is easy to lecture on ways to organize peer commentary sessions, but implementing the idea with secondary students is a whole different ball game. The same disconnect was present with the idea of coaching student-writers. We could easily role-play coaching skills with each other in the pre-service teachers' class, but it would not be authentic. The writing center would remedy this challenge. We would take our knowledge on-site, get real-world practice, and reflect on the experiences. The writing center would enable us to have real conversations with students, and although there would be challenges that would arise (much like the realities of any secondary classroom), we were optimistic that the grounded instruction the pre-service teachers received in their Teaching Composition 7–12 course would enable them to develop the "teacher's gut" in deciding how to proceed.

The writing center would provide a unique opportunity where I, a teacher-educator, and my students, pre-service teachers, could be absorbed into the students' school and lives. We planned to aid students seeking help with their writing in various ways. Childers, Fels, and Jordan (2004) offered a list of objectives that mirrored those of our center:

- Create opportunities for individualized writing conferences.
- Reinforce writing as a process.
- Improve writing when writers focus on the writing—not the grade.
- Support classroom activities.
- Create an environment where writers can bounce ideas off others, questions can lead to new ideas, writing for self or publication can blossom, and resources on writing abound.

We aimed to create a positive, structured environment where both the secondary students and pre-service teachers could develop their skills and knowledge. This comfortable space would focus on writing, and although the climate would be welcoming, we wanted to be sure that it would be a working place that focuses on writing—not simply a place to hang out or escape from class. Coaching writing would also help the pre-service teachers by helping them become better communicators, putting their ideas into practice, and helping them gain confidence as writing coaches and writing teachers.

FINDING THE RIGHT SCHOOL FOR THE WRITING CENTER

Initially, we realized that the school chosen as the home for our writing center would have to be in close proximity to our college campus since many of our college students utilized public transportation, carpooled, or rode their bicycles to class. The first secondary school we approached about the idea of creating a writing center was within walking distance of campus. We did not end up working with this school, however, because of difficulty in scheduling meetings with the principal. We realized that we would not be able to obtain adequate support for our venture if the administration was too busy to have an initial meeting with us.

The second school that we approached was in a different neighborhood but within 2 miles of our campus. The principal agreed to meet with us and also pulled together several faculty members for our initial meeting. We presented our ideas and objectives to the group, answered questions about the project, and finally shook hands. Our collaboration was set to begin at the start of the coming school year.

Our writing center opened in the fall of 2007 in an urban high school. At the time, the school had close to 1,000 students and was known for low test scores. Because of this, the school was not making Adequate Yearly Progress (AYP) and had recently undergone a restructuring plan in which a new principal had been hired and all faculty members had to re-interview in order to keep their teaching positions. Half of the faculty returned the following year. Even though we entered the school shortly after this time of turmoil, it ended up being an opportune time to join the school community. With over one-half of the faculty being new, we were joining *their* ranks and were presented as part of the school landscape. One challenge, however, was that there were many new programs on the horizon at the high school, so we

> **We did not want to simply be there for a semester or year; instead, we aimed to become an integral part of the school climate.**

began outreach efforts immediately to get to know the students and faculty. We wanted all high school faculty to clearly know that this was a service project with pre-service teachers and college faculty donating their time and energy to be in the school to support student-writers. It was also important to us to build a sustainable program. We did not want to simply be there for a semester or year; instead, we aimed to become an integral part of the school climate.

Administrative support and a viable space are two key elements in developing a center. The new principal was not only open to the idea of establishing a secondary writing center on site, but she was enthusiastic and incredibly supportive as well. We were given a spacious room in the freshman wing.

All workers in the writing center were volunteers: College faculty donated their time, former English education students sought additional experience, and one section of a Teaching Composition 7–12 course was held on-site. Students in this course had the option of completing a service learning final project that involved volunteering in the center. Pre-service teachers in the Teaching Composition 7–12 course would be able to directly apply the methods they learned through coursework to their coaching experiences in the writing center. Readings and training activities in the Teaching Composition 7–12 course enabled the pre-service teachers to not only discuss the coaching methods but to gain experience working through the process before they worked with secondary students.

We focused our coaching practice on Donald Murray's (2004) approach, which he described in his classic text *A Writer Teaches Writing*:

1. The student comments on the draft.
2. The teacher reads or reviews the draft.
3. The teacher responds to the student's comments.
4. The student responds to the teacher's response (p. 148).

We chose to study Murray's text because of his emphasis on the student's agency in the process of writing. We did not aspire to dominate the conversations with students; instead, it was our hope that they would absorb the skills and strategies shared during the writing conference and make them part of their writing process.

The pre-service teachers had the opportunity to help set up the room, which was excellent practice for them in organizing their own future classrooms. The numerous hours it took them to seek donations, clean the room, and set up the center also taught them how time-consuming and labor-intensive their work would be.

We strove to be open-minded to all possibilities for interaction with the students. We wanted to support the teachers and students in whatever ways they needed regarding improvement in writing. Secondary students could come to the center on a drop-in basis, as members of small groups, or as an entire class. The writing center staff would also go into classrooms in order to provide mini-lessons, in-class instructional support, and small-group coaching opportunities. When we opened, we felt prepared and simply did what other writing center staff members do: We waited for the secondary students to arrive. And they did, but slowly; during the first week of operation, we conferenced with four students. But as word began to spread, we saw more students and received more repeat business. Numbers for the first 2 months totaled 103 visits (84 individual conferences and one class visit with 19 students). In the spring term, the writing center expanded its hours. Contact steadily grew and then exploded. In the month of February, for instance, our student contacts were over 500: 66 individual conferences, 18 classroom visits to the center and in-class instructional support (192 students), five tours (46 students), one grade-level presentation (120 students), one book club session (15 students), and one Manga presentation (65 students). Clearly, our writing center was becoming foundational to literacy instruction in this struggling school.

Special events and activities offered through the center helped ensure that the facility's services reached a large number of students. We not only wanted to continue outreach efforts, but these events helped our aim of building a sustainable program. One such activity was an annual fall writing contest that celebrated student writing. Pre-service teachers obtained donations from college faculty and community members to fund the contest awards, and we were able to disperse nearly 10 awards in different genres of writing. The winners accompanied the pre-service teachers to the college campus to have a tour, eat lunch in the union, and spend their gift cards in a downtown bookstore. Another extension activity was the monthly Brown Bag Book Club. I obtained a grant to help support the venture. The book club's motto was catchy: Free Book, Free Pizza, Free Conversation. The once-a-month gathering soon drew nearly 25 members, who had the opportunity to talk about books with college students over their lunch hour.

An online tutoring option was developed by the pre-service teachers as well, so the secondary students could submit their writing for feedback via email. Students would receive a reply with feedback from a writing coach within 48 hours. Additionally, we ended the first year by holding a festive Celebration of Writers breakfast with a hot meal and handmade awards. The breakfast celebration was held in order to replace a district writing competition that had lost its funding. All of these activities not only promoted the writing center but also allowed volunteers to make meaningful connections with students and helped establish our presence in the school as a place that supports students' literacy skills. We had, indeed, become a part of the school's literacy landscape.

PRE-SERVICE TEACHERS' EXPERIENCES
IN THE WRITING CENTER

It was vitally important to conduct research on the writing center in order to ascertain what the pre-service teachers specifically gained from the experience. I was hoping that the results would also give us insight into ways to improve our center and yield data that we could use to garner more support for the initiative in our college. Data was gathered in the spring term of 2007 through a focus-group interview, reflective journals, and an online survey. A colleague in the secondary education department led the focus group and also helped code and organize the data. The research questions included:

- Before your experience here, what was your view of writing centers?
- How has that view changed?
- What are some of the things you have worked on as a writing coach through the writing center?
- What are some of the victories you have experienced?
- What are some of the challenges you have faced as a writing coach?
- Considering your experiences with students . . .
  » What are you learning?
  » What are you getting better at?
  » What do you still like to work on?

- What connections can be made from your experiences to the content of ENG4620 Teaching Composition 7–12?
- What are the biggest things from this experience that you will take into your future classroom?

It is important to note that when the writing center opened, not all of the pre-service teachers were familiar with the concept of a writing center. One-third either did not know such centers existed or did not know they existed at the secondary level. Two-thirds thought that the purpose of writing centers was to offer extra help such as tutoring or editing, particularly for students who were not good writers.

These findings made it clear that the prospective teachers were exposed to new ideas and concepts through the year. Other striking themes emerged from the data collected from the center's pre-service teachers. These individuals mentioned the writing environment, motivation for writing, the writing process, and specific skills that they acquired through the experience. While these pre-service teachers were still learning the "rules of the game," the information they provided is relevant to veteran writing teachers and teacher educators as well, for the responses are a reminder of the key principles of effective writing instruction.

The Writing Environment

Many pre-service teachers mentioned that the environment of the writing center had a positive impact on the success of the students. In particular, they noted that the writing center was a quiet place where students could work and focus on their writing. One pre-service teacher characterized the center as "a place where you can come to get your thoughts clear in a quiet place to write . . . . Most students won't have that." Another remarked that "It's kind of a quiet place where they can escape from the rest of the day." Yet another observed that "Some students come to the writing center to find a quiet, safe place to think and compose, so the tutor needs to know when to back off and create the peaceful space."

In *Teaching English Creatively* (2001), John H. Bushman stressed the power of the physical, emotional, and intellectual aspects of classroom climate. Bushman and Jim Blasingame also emphasized climate in their textbook *Teaching Writing in Middle and Secondary Schools* (Blasingame & Bushman, 2005), devoting the entire first chapter to the topic. They wrote,

> A positive classroom climate is a must if young adults are to function in a writing program that involves personal risk. Students, who place their thoughts on paper for all to see, need to be in a supportive environment. Writing, like all other important activities, involves risk if we do it well. (p. 2)

As writing coaches supporting writing instruction throughout the school, we focused on creating an environment that was welcoming and comforting in appearance and emotion, and we assured students that the center was a place where every individual was an active participant in his or her own learning.

Issues of school climate also affected the pre-service teachers. The site offered many of the college students the opportunity to experience a school culture that they had not previously encountered. The at-risk school environment was something about which they reflected:

> I have come to find that (this high school) is a wonderful place, and that I wouldn't mind teaching in an environment like this. . . . As you walk down the halls, the students that you judge as thugs are the ones that would happily show you where to go to find what you need, and they are the ones that welcome you into the school with a friendly nod or hello in passing.

There were some obstacles to creating a positive climate in the writing center. One challenge noted by the pre-service teachers was that not all students came willingly. In some cases, students were sent to the writing center as *punishment*. Although this problem was addressed (and possibly solved) by working with teachers to ensure that students are sent to the writing center with an understanding of our writing center aims, the experience stuck with some of the pre-service teachers. One explained,

> Some students come to the writing center because their content teacher doesn't know what else to do with them, so the tutor needs to engage the displaced students in an activity that builds the students' confidence and doesn't make the writing center seem like a place of punishment.

We strove to work with students by first connecting with them, then focusing on their writing. Although we never encouraged teachers to send students to the writing center as punishment, the pre-service teacher staff felt that they worked to establish a bond with these individuals, so the experience was not perceived as punishment in the end.

Some of the pre-service teachers took strong emotions or feelings about public perceptions of the school away from the experience. Since our secondary school is considered an at-risk school, many of the pre-service teachers reflected on how one person can make a difference. One wrote:

> I bet a lot of people out there in the community who don't believe in this school wouldn't believe that writing came from within its walls. These students have shown me what amazing things high school students can produce when motivated, encouraged, and supported.

It seems that the writing center experience has definitely made an impression on many of the pre-service teachers and possibly broke down some of their perceptions regarding what failing schools in urban areas may look like. This ties back to the individuality of our approach—each assignment, student, and experience is different. Our job was to make connections with the students and make a difference in the school, and our service-learning approach was certainly helping us achieve that.

It is not always easy to decipher what pre-service teachers take away from a field experience, for they don't always give adequate reflection of what they are truly absorbing in the classroom setting. Therefore, some of the questions in the focus group addressed this topic. One student summed up the experience quite succinctly: "I learned to praise often, listen a lot, be willing to learn from each session, not judge other teachers, and not pre-judge the student—no matter what their background."

The Value of Coaching Individual Writers

Some pre-service teachers referred to the writing process throughout the interview, survey, and reflective journal. They expressed an understanding that writing is a process and emphasized the fact that students can come to the writing center and get help at any time during this process. This same idea is supported by Murray (2004): "We do not teach writing effectively if we try to make all students and all writing the same" (p. 5). The ultimate goal of tutoring was to help students become independent writers and aid them in recognizing their process and what works for them. Even though these college students had long been utilizing the process in their own academic work, teaching the process to students seemed to change their perceptions of it. One pre-service teacher commented, "Now I understand . . . that [conferencing] is a tool that students can use at any point in the writing process." Another saw the value in one-on-one coaching "help(ing) at any point during the writing process."

The pre-service teachers had read Murray's (2004) ideas about conferencing and had also role-played different tutoring scenarios. Murray believed that "Conference teaching is the most effective—and the most practical—method of teaching composition" (p. 147). The power of the individual teaching conference gave the pre-service teachers practice with this technique. The pre-service teachers learned that asking good questions is not the only key to success, for the skill of listening carefully to the student responses is also important. Through the writing center experience, many of the pre-service teachers felt that they had greatly improved in this area. Listening also helps to ensure that a coach does not dominate the conversation. In the words of one pre-service teacher:

Probably one of the biggest lessons I will take with me to my classroom, though, is to sit back, shut up, and let the students direct their education as much as they can. I've learned to not barge in and take charge of sessions, but to instead let the students tell me what they want or feel they need to work on.

Murray continually stressed that the conversation between a teacher and a student should be focused on what the student has to say. In order to create such a conversation, it is imperative that teachers learn how to ask the secondary students effective questions in order to get them thinking critically about their own writing. In essence, the teacher must strive to figure out what students need, according to one study participant. Another writing coach underscores the importance of "asking questions and then dealing with the answers you get and then knowing where to go with the answers and how to generate more questions, so it feels that it's student-led interaction."

In his textbook *What's the Big Idea? Question-Driven Units to Motivate Reading, Writing, and Thinking*, Jim Burke (2010) noted that questioning is as old as Socrates, who used questions to obtain deeper knowledge. Burke observed that "As students learn . . . questions—or, in some instances, sets of questions—they develop an independence of mind—an intellectual facility that serves them well whether reading or writing, researching or presenting, evaluating or analyzing, comparing or contrasting" (p. 12). Questions are important in writing conferences as well, for they challenge the student to think through their own aims, processes, and obstacles. Modeling this questioning hopefully will transfer to their secondary students' own processes of thinking about writing in the future.

> **With a little guidance and well-designed questions to get them thinking critically, I can scaffold students until they realize that they do indeed possess the tools to produce a quality piece of writing.**

Pre-service teachers explained that the process of coaching had improved their own question asking abilities, which helped them provide a focus for writing conferences. "I'm getting better at asking direct questions," one began, "that either lead a student to think or solve an issue they may have in their writing or writing questions that help me decide what sort of help they need."

Becoming comfortable with and adept at the process of questioning often requires practice. As one pre-service teacher said, "The more experience you have, the more you learn what situations call for what kinds of questions." Because of this, the role of questioning can help pre-service teachers see the place of the writing conference within the writing process itself: "With a little guidance and well-designed questions to get them thinking critically, I can scaffold students until they realize that they do indeed possess the tools to produce a quality piece of writing."

The Value of Patience and Motivation

For novice teachers, it can be tempting to rush through a process or lesson plan. These pre-service teachers were no exception. Patience emerged as an issue that affected all the pre-service teachers during their experience. As one noted, "Patience, just patience all around . . . whatever comes to you in the classroom, whatever comes to you in the writing center . . . just try to be as patient as possible." Another added,

> I would agree with patience. The biggest things I learned here from tutoring is that there are going to be some students who resist you the entire time, and really, all you can do is be patient and continue to encourage them and get them as far as you can and don't take it personally if they don't do it.

Some of the pre-service teachers expressed that patience involves more than simply working with one student—it involves the spectrum of writing experiences one will have in the classroom. One pre-service teacher reflected, "Students will more often than not be at different levels in their writing, and I need to be patient with all of those different learners. . . ." One student noted that the patience she gained through her tutoring experiences would serve her well in her teaching career. She admitted, "I learned some valuable lessons this semester; mostly that I am more patient than I knew. I need to have more confidence in my knowledge."

When asked to describe some of the things they had worked on as coaches in the writing center that connected to their collegiate coursework, the pre-service teachers mentioned the following: topic generation, pre-writing, outlining, free writing, organizing papers, helping English Language Learners, revision, and deciphering teacher expectations for the assignment. The majority of the pre-service teachers mentioned one key component that tied all of these together: motivation. As one noted, "Give them [secondary students] a reason to care." Another college student reflected that there must be "a better way to really motivate reluctant learners."

Motivation can be linked to classroom climate and the physical, emotional, and intellectual elements of the classroom. For the pre-service teachers, concerns about motivation involved trying to coach students on the spot: How could a tutor get a student to care about an assignment? What pre-writing activities could a tutor suggest that might inspire a student to find the right topic? In addition, the pre-service teachers recognized that it was important that they not do the work for the secondary students. As one noted, "Some students just want someone else to do the work for them, so a writing center tutor has to persuade them to take ownership and responsibility."

The Importance of Clear Expectations

The Teaching Composition 7–12 course at our university offers pre-service teachers instruction and practice creating assignment sheets and rubrics for writing assignments. However, a common problem we encountered in the writing center was a lack of understanding of writing assignment instructions; this was true for both students and writing coaches. Although having assignment sheets or rubrics would have greatly alleviated this problem, the students' lack of comprehension of their assignments (caused either by absences or a general lack of understanding) remained a challenge throughout the year. Motivating and working with students who did not have a clear concept of what to do was a stumbling block for many of the pre-service teachers, who sometimes found that "[the student] had no idea what [they were] doing." Thus, it appears that the value of having clear expectations for students via writing assignment sheets and rubrics is something the pre-service teachers will take with them to their future classrooms.

LESSONS LEARNED BY PRE-SERVICE TEACHERS

Through the interviews conducted with our tutors, it became clear that the pre-service teachers would take much of what they learned at the writing center into their future classrooms. One individual wrote that she had learned to "fry the big fish and let the little ones slip away sometimes—in other words, focus on the most important elements of an assignment so the grader and the student are not overwhelmed by the minutiae." Other pre-service teachers claimed to have developed new knowledge. One pre-service teacher remarked:

> We are teaching students to make connections, even in their writing. I need to continue to make connections as well. Everything I am learning, even in my other classes, are parts of the puzzle. The writing center has given me the opportunity to pull what I am learning in class and see how it fits together in the lives of actual students who just want to be themselves.

Other pre-service teachers expressed that the experience had deepened knowledge they had previously gained:

> Writing has always come easily to me, so I needed this experience
> to understand how intimidated some students are by a blank piece
> of paper. I think I had never considered that I would have to *teach*
> students to write. Somehow, I thought merely explaining the structure
> of paragraphs and essays and reading different genres to see how they
> are constructed would be different. I was dead wrong and am so glad to
> have learned it before I had students of my own.

The data seems to show that our Teaching Composition 7–12 course content is strong. What our pre-service teachers needed, however, was the opportunity to practice these ideas, experience firsthand the challenges and joys of working with student-writers, and then to reflect on those experiences.

All teachers must continue to reflect and learn throughout their careers. One of the pre-service teachers highlighted this point:

> The most important thing I will take is that in teaching writing, I have
> to be a learner and doer of writing. I need to use the writing process
> even when I am creating assignments, and I need to make sure that
> assignments and lessons are all connected for myself and my students.

It certainly appears that the pre-service teachers who coached student-writers in the writing center will continue to learn throughout their careers. Monica Techau, who volunteered in the center for nearly 2 years and currently teaches at Sky Vista Middle School in Aurora, Colorado, noted the following:

> The Writing Center (WC) was absolutely essential to my development
> as a teacher. It provided me with multiple opportunities to work side-
> by-side with students, which in turn allowed me to become more
> and more comfortable in the teacher role prior to even beginning my
> career as a teacher. I gained confidence in my ability to actually help
> students! Now, when a paper is put in front of me and a voice mumbles,
> "I need help with this," I don't feel overwhelmed. The need to look at
> EVERYTHING has been eliminated due to my time at the WC, where
> I realized that trying to take on every single strength and weakness in
> a student's writing is actually a disservice. They become overwhelmed
> (and so do I!). Asking clear questions about what stage of writing the
> student is at and what exactly they're wanting or needing help with
> is key. Just as key as not accepting, "I need help with everything."
> :) I learned how to do this through the writing center. (personal
> communication, May 1, 2010)

Another current teacher and former volunteer in the writing center, Carolyn Chase, agrees. Chase, who currently teaches at Lakewood High School in Lakewood, Colorado (which has its own secondary writing center), noted that

> Our goal is to help the writer take ownership of their writing. I offer open-ended extra credit for my own students to go to the writing lab for help (hopefully before they turn a piece of writing in, but I encourage them to go after as well to revise) and instruct them, with my early writing center experiences in mind, to come with questions about their writing prepared. I expect my students to be the captains of their own writing and remind them that they are not to show up and say, "This is bad, fix it," or "Edit this, please!" I know the writing center is there to offer support and guidance, but ultimately the goal is confident independence. (personal communication, July 10, 2010)

Jeremiah Quinonez is another former writing center pre-service teacher. He now teaches English as a Second Language and English at Bear Creek High School in Lakewood, Colorado. Quinonez clearly saw the value in his experience coaching student-writers in the writing center:

> Writing centers are places where tutors and teachers have ample time to assess needs, answer questions, explore options, and exchange feedback with students. While assisting as a writing center coach, I was astounded by the confidence and success generated by the one-on-one interaction. Students left with a renewed sense of direction and self-efficacy. (personal communication, July 1, 2010)

Quinonez went on to note the benefits he saw to the students learning the English language:

> As an ESL teacher, I have also found that writing centers offer a wealth of support for second language learners. While simultaneously learning academic content and a new language, English Language Learners require the extra guidance and support that many if not most teachers are unable to provide because of time constraints. My writing center experiences enabled me to see the transformation in my students, both in their papers and in their eyes. I realized that their time in the writing center could have been the stepping-stone between failure and success.

Clearly, these new teaching professionals took their pre-service writing center experiences to their current classrooms, where they noticed how coaching student-writers influenced their teaching.

LESSONS FOR A TEACHER-EDUCATOR
AND WRITING CENTER DIRECTOR

As a teacher-educator and writing center director, I have learned a great deal as well. First, it is incredibly important to have a well-defined vision throughout the process of creating and sustaining a writing center. Having this strong foundation of knowledge was essential initially, for early choices relied heavily upon informed decision making built on writing center research and pedagogy. When stumbling blocks occurred, it was imperative to refer back to our vision, for the aim and goals of our project helped see us through both good and tough times.

Administrative support—on both the secondary and collegiate levels—is also a key component of success. Even though we weren't burdened with a budget, administrators' support of the time it took for us to initialize our project was critical to our success. Providing frequent updates to administrators at the high school and our college showcased our progress and efforts, and it also became fodder for future endeavors. Additionally, it is vital to have colleague support, for this is a project that is not easily done solo. Finding one who truly cares about the center and can assist when needed is imperative in order not to feel that the entire world rests on one person's shoulders. Success doesn't come down to one individual—it comes down to the team that works together.

Allowing time for the project to take hold is another important consideration. It is a bit like the movie *Field of Dreams* (Robinson, 1989): "If you build it, they will come." They will, but it may take a while. This is not necessarily a negative thing, for the time that you have initially will enable policies and practices to take hold before the rush comes in. As time passes, extension opportunities (such as book clubs, writing contests, and poetry workshops) arise. Planning those extra activities is a great way to spend the downtime in the writing center. These extensions come from the secondary students' hearts—it is what you sense will enhance their learning, their days, their lives. These same opportunities also give the pre-service teachers the opportunity to broaden their experiences while expanding the writing center's services and outreach to the school community. Those outreach efforts bring more individuals into the writing center.

Creating the writing center greatly benefited me as an educator. I saw the content of my Teaching Composition course come alive. I had the opportunity to be next to my pre-service teachers and was able to guide them (as much as they needed) during their coaching experiences. I was also lucky to be able to converse with them after their coaching sessions to discuss challenges and accomplishments. So even though the service project of creating a secondary writing project took much time and effort, it paid off double-fold. I know my pre-service teachers have become better instructors because of their writing center experiences, and they are able to recognize this, too.

Finally, in true service-learning projects, it is important that both groups benefit from the experience. During the past 3 years, we have had contact with more than 3,000 students. Previous activities such as the Brown Bag Book Club continue, as do services we provided in the past. Writing scores at the school have slightly improved, and even though there is no specific evidence to directly support our impact on those improvements, I am sure that our work had a positive influence. It also now seems that the writing center is a permanent part of the school landscape. It is of paramount importance to have a sustainable program. Since it takes time for a project like this to evolve, those involved must be in it for the long haul.

FINAL THOUGHTS

We have much more to learn in order to sustain our growth and refine our practices at the writing center. We know that we will face new challenges each year. Currently, we are dealing with infusing writing instruction into a tightly structured curriculum that follows a strict sequence of instruction. Teachers feel pressured to keep in line with the tight calendar, which leaves them less likely to have time to utilize some of our services. We are also dealing with school renovation, which requires us to share our space and to constantly introduce ourselves to new students, faculty, and administration.

Overcoming challenges is something we also model for our pre-service teachers, because we know that overcoming obstacles is something they will do throughout their teaching careers and because we have evidence that we are making a difference. As Monica Techau noted,

> As a teacher, I try to have as many real-world models as possible for whatever task we are taking on. The WC provided me with multiple models every day for both the students as they see other kids working on their writing and for the pre-service teachers as we observe teachers working with students, what types of questions they're asking, and how to create an environment of rigorous writing. The countless benefits of my experience with the urban high school WC leave me with one question, "Why wouldn't I start a WC at my school?" (personal communication, May 1, 2010)

That question points to the promise of a program like ours to pre-service teachers and teacher-educators. As the teachers who describe their pre-service experiences show here, their work in the writing center complemented their classroom experience in such a way to prepare them for the real experiences teachers have. It also prepared them to start writing centers in schools where they begin their teaching careers.

Teacher-educators hoping to transform English education students' field experiences need look no further than the high school writing center. The first step is to determine the needs of pre-service teachers and then to design plans for collaborating with an area school that either has or hopes to have a writing center. As our example shows, collaboration simply starts with a phone call and conversations about how the program can be used to benefit the pre-service teachers, the high school students, and the high school faculty. Time is needed to set up and sustain a center if there isn't one, so it is important to have plenty of support for the program and realistic goals for how and when to open the center. Though financial backing is not necessary to set up or sustain a writing center, there are state and federal grants available that support service-learning projects, especially if those projects are designed to boost student achievement in underperforming schools. Finally, program assessment that is rooted in feedback from everyone involved is critical to the program's success and sustainability. Assessment helps in determining whether initial program goals were met. Pre-service teachers, students, teachers, the teacher-educator(s), and writing center director(s) supervising the program should all contribute to its assessment. Their reflections should provide a basis for planning how the program will be extended into the future, so that the writing center and pre-service experience can become part of the school's landscape and part of the pre-service teachers' training.

What began as an interest in offering pre-service teachers more authentic teaching experiences has now grown into an integral part of our Teaching Composition course. Pre-service teachers know about the activity and look forward to the contact time with secondary students. The keys to success have been to be flexible (in order to meet the needs of both the pre-service teachers and secondary students), to maintain a positive presence at the school, and to utilize the service-learning model. Without this model, we would not be sustainable, and we plan on being involved at the school for many years to come.

REFERENCES

Blasingame, J., & Bushman, J. H. (2005). *Teaching writing in middle and secondary schools.* Upple Saddle River, NJ: Pearson.

Burke, J. (2010). *What's the big idea? Question-driven units to motivate reading, writing, and thinking.* Portsmouth, NH: Heinemann.

Bushman, J. H. (2001). *Teaching English creatively.* Springfield, IL: Charles C. Thomas, Publisher.

Childers, P. B., Fels, D., & Jordan, J. (2004, Fall). The secondary school writing center: A place to build confident, competent writers. *Praxis: A Writing Center Journal 2*(1). Retrieved from http://projects.uwc.utexas.edu/praxis/?q=node/91

Eby, J. W. (1998, March). *Why service-learning is bad.* Retrieved from http://www.messiah.edu/external_programs/agape/servicelearning/articles/wrongsvc.pdf

Eyler, J., & Giles, D. E. (1999). *Where's the learning in service-learning?* San Francisco: Jossey-Bass Publishers.

Learn and Serve America. (n.d.). *What is service-learning?* Retrieved from National Service Learning Clearinghouse website: http://www.servicelearning.org/what_is_service-learning

Murray, D. (2004). *A writer teaches writing* (2nd ed.). Boston: Heinle-Thomson.

Robinson, P. A. (Director). (1989). *Field of dreams* [Motion Picture]. USA: Universal Studios.

CHAPTER NINE

What State Auditors Taught Me About Writing Center Evaluation

Dawn Fels

This chapter offers readers a view of writing center evaluation that celebrates the myriad ways writing centers can lead collaborative literacy education within school communities. Since the enactment of No Child Left Behind (NCLB) in 2002, public schools in particular have labored to meet demands that have left teachers and students weary—and wary—of evaluation. The milieu in which high school writing centers exist today is peppered with rhetoric about *failing teachers* and *failing schools*. Intellectual freedom, identities, futures, and, as we are learning—health and well-being—are all at risk. Smyth (2008) cited more than 20 studies that tie high-stakes testing to anxiety, low self-concept, anger, and fear of failure in students as young as elementary school, feelings also held by teachers. As Smyth's article indicates, the body of scholarship about the effects of NCLB on teaching and learning has widened and now includes scholars in a variety of related fields: school administration, assessment, special education, urban education, higher education, school psychology, English education, teachers of English to speakers of other languages, and cultural studies. Scholars in each field describe their concerns with the law's effects on students, especially those students whom the law was designed to protect: rural and urban students; linguistic, cultural, ethnic, and racial minorities; students living in poverty; and students with disabilities. While the scholarship reports many of the realities that teachers and students face, its purpose is to inform. But if reform is the goal, nothing beats the local efforts of teachers, students, and community members. A writing center can serve as a hub for their efforts and use evaluation to trumpet their success.

State and federal mandates create several opportunities for writing center directors to use evaluation more wisely to support local literacy education efforts. In her address to attendees of the Midwest Writing Centers Association in 2007, Kathleen Blake Yancey praised writing centers as "the most important unit" in helping students transfer literacies between and among the many communities to which they belong. She encouraged writing center directors in both universities and K–12 schools to create not for but *with* students a writing center that can become that one place to which students return throughout their school careers to develop essential academic, interpersonal, and technological skills. For secondary school writing center directors, this also means creating for and with members of the school community an evaluation system that not only unblocks their center's potential (Grimm, 2003) but advocates for teachers and students. Writing center evaluation should showcase the achievements of both teachers and students: academic, public, professional, creative, intellectual, and imaginative. Writing center evaluation should focus on how members of the school community come together to *do* literacy. This chapter offers insight into how to do that.

EXPLAINING WHAT WRITING CENTERS DO

In 2001, I set up a writing center in a school where I taught English. I started from scratch with only my experience as a graduate student tutor in a university writing center. Because so many new directors believe money is the key to launching a successful center, I started by scouring the Internet for sources of funding. No luck. I set up shop in the only space available—my classroom. Because the room only had three walls at the time and overlooked the library and a noisy hallway, this was not the quiet, reflective place I envisioned for our writing center, but I seized the opportunity to make it work. With no budget for new furniture, I scavenged discarded pieces found in the hallways. I hauled up from the cafeteria a menagerie of orange, white, and yellow plastic chairs whose scale and modern design clashed with the room's heavy seminar tables.

Once the room was put together, I shifted my attention to the documents that would anchor our work: a proposal, a mission, and a guiding philosophy. I wrote these from what I knew about writing center and composition theories, describing in detail how we would work (and not work) and how tutors would be selected and trained. I even worked with a graphic designer who donated time to create a funky logo for our center; it figured prominently on the triplicate report form I designed and ordered from the print shop. We opened our doors in November with an initial tutoring staff comprised of teachers from across the disciplines, parents, retired educators, professional writers, business leaders, freelance writers, college professors, graduate students, and friends of friends.

Within months, we realized we had a lot to celebrate. Our initial staff of 20 writing coaches logged an astonishing 500 sessions with more than 350 students, just over one-third of our student body. Several teachers brought their classes down to the center for workshops and small-group tutoring. Two local newspapers carried stories about our writing center, which one reporter called "unusual" in a school like ours, and in November 2001, three colleagues and I took our center's story to a national conference where we shared our students' and colleagues' testimonials, captured on video by freelance filmmakers who donated their time and services. The following year, we added peer tutors to our team of writing coaches who tutored alongside community members, parents, faculty, and college students. We had a lot to celebrate, indeed, as the story of our center made its way from our suburban city across the metropolitan area to writing center colleagues across the country. But there was one group with whom we did not anticipate sharing our pride: the state auditors.

> **If reform is the goal, nothing beats the local efforts of teachers, students, and community members. A writing center can serve as a hub for their efforts and use evaluation to trumpet their success.**

In 2002, our high school was among the first public schools in our area to feel the pinch of NCLB. We were named a *school of concern*, and our writing center was listed among the interventions on our school improvement plans. Our entire faculty and student body prepared for the state auditing team's visit, and I anticipated auditors' requests to see evidence of how the center improved student achievement. Although I stood by our writing center's work, my greatest fear was that auditors might ask if visits to the writing center led to improvement in students' test scores. I also worried that I would say something that might portray the writing center as a remedial site or further misrepresent our school. My concerns grew out of what I was told—that the auditors were there to find evidence of *failure*.

But once they arrived, it became clear that no one expected to see a writing center in a school like ours. Most of the auditors were unfamiliar with the writing center concept entirely. *What does a writing center do?* they asked. After offering a brief explanation of our pedagogical approach, I turned to what I thought might impress them: data about the number of sessions logged, how many students were repeat users, how many teachers held workshops in the center. The longer I spoke, the more their heads nodded. The more they nodded, the greater grew my fear of the inevitable question about writing center work and test scores. Hoping to divert the auditors' attention away from quantifiable "proof" of our center's role in boosting student achievement, I started telling stories about our students and tutors. I also introduced the auditors to students, peer tutors, teachers, and volunteers available in the writing center at the time. Each told a different story about the writing center's critical role in teaching, learning, and community building. They told stories about how peer tutors and teachers worked together to tutor individuals and small groups; how poor kids from the 'hood taught the college kids about life and privilege; how retired educators worked alongside parents, tutoring students who were not their students, teenagers who were not their teenagers; and how university professors modeled for their pre-service teachers how and why they should work with struggling students.

Each year for 3 years, the auditors heard new stories. A teacher who volunteered as a writing coach during her planning period talked about the value of listening to students and the need to put down the red pen. A student who was a talented artist with dyslexia, who gave up on writing in middle school, credited a tutor for helping her find confidence as a writer and a new way to illustrate her art. A 30-year veteran teacher said that what she witnessed in the writing center changed the way she taught. A first-year teacher said she *actually* looked forward to reading 120 students' essays. We also told stories about our efforts to effect change in the school's reading and writing culture. We told them how all faculty, peer tutors, and volunteer tutors were trained together in our writing center pedagogy. We pointed to how this enabled teachers from across the curriculum to use our writing center pedagogy in their classrooms or to join in as a tutor when they brought their classes down for small-group tutoring. We described Partners in Print, a program that paired a volunteer reading partner from among our peer tutors, faculty, or community members with a ninth-grader who read far below grade level; together, the pair chose a novel to read from among a set of books purchased with grant money. We shared stories of how other peer tutors, accomplished artists, photographers, creative writers, and essayists made perfect assistants to the faculty advisor of the school's literary magazine. The tutors' suggestions to expand beyond the typical written texts (poetry and short fiction) to include students' original photographs and artwork, essays, collaborative pieces, and personal statements not only made for a literary magazine that better reflected the diverse literacy talents of our student body but netted us a blue ribbon in NCTE's annual contest for high school literary magazines. Teachers and community members who played critical roles in our center's launch and later success were nominated (and subsequently won) school district awards for their service. Teacher-colleagues continued to volunteer their time as tutors, and some took up pens of a different sort as participants in a creative writing group for teachers (see Fels, 2008).

These and other unforeseen outcomes of our writing center's work impressed the state auditors. Our writing center served as a hub for success stories that stood in direct contrast with the narrative formed by our *failing* status. Once we had a chance to show the auditors what we did, how valuable our one-to-one pedagogy was for all involved, I realized that proof of our writing center's efficacy could not be found among the columns on the spreadsheet.

WRITING CENTERS AND TEST SCORES

School accreditation carries with it a whole host of institutional goals to which the writing center contributes. Improving test scores, however, should not be one of them. If writing centers' primary role is to help students hone multiple literacies while keeping writing instruction student-centered, focusing on test scores would create a rhetorical realm around writing center evaluation that "signal[s] what is to be said and what is not to be said" (Villanueva, 2006, p. 5). What needs to be said is that agreeing to show how writing center visits lead to improvement in test scores—though they may—will change the nature of writing centers and eventually prove lethal to the relationships writing centers have with teachers and students. We need to move forward, not backwards, in our advocacy work on behalf of teachers and students. Writing centers cannot advocate for teachers and students if they are complicit in a process that misrepresents them.

> Writing center evaluation can explore how work in and through the center contributes to accreditation benchmark data in ways that, when reported, does not lead to further mislabeling of teachers and students.

Writing centers can, however, explore how work in and through the center contributes to improvements in accreditation benchmark data that, when reported, does not lead to further mislabeling of teachers and students. For instance, what might our center contribute to teachers' professional development? Do students who struggle to attend school regularly keep appointments with tutors? How might help in the writing center encourage students to stay in school and graduate? How many at-risk students or first-generation students attribute their decisions to attend college to the help and encouragement of a writing center tutor? What benefits do tutors glean from their work? In what ways has the writing center served the individual needs of students with disabilities? English Language Learners? Having answers to these questions not only serves the writing center's interests but institutional goals, as well.

SEARCHING FOR SUCCESS BEYOND THE STATISTICS

The overreliance on statistical representations of writing center work has been the subject of several articles and book chapters written over the years by writing center scholars. Boquet, Grimm, and Lerner have all argued for more authentic depictions of the writing center's role in teaching and learning that align more closely with the center's mission. Boquet (2002) asserted that the focus of writing center research should be on what happens between tutor and student—not the data we think will impress administrators. The tutoring session is about much more than the number of sessions held each day or over the course of the year, the number of minutes tutors spend tutoring, the number of students they can see during their shifts, or the lists of strategies they encourage students to try. Similarly, students' needs are much more complex than statistics can convey.

How does one quantify, for example, a student's anxiety about writing a college essay, or an essay on a topic they consider religiously taboo, or one that brings back memories of a traumatic event? What data field fully describes the experience of a student whose learning disability brings them to the writing center for help decoding class notes? For organizing ideas for a paper? For understanding the texts on which a writing assignment is based? Where on the reports do we identify the needs of the blind student who comes to the center to have their exams read to them? The student with Asperger's who finds it easier to talk out their text to a tutor who types it? How do statistical methods of record keeping communicate the frustrations and successes of a ninth-grader reading at a third-grade level? How do we objectify the good news? The pride of a student who won an essay contest? The gratitude of a student who just wants to thank a tutor for spending that extra time with them? The former tutor, now graduated, who comes back to visit and reminisce during their winter break? All of these connections merit more than a click on a drop-down field.

But interactions like these among students and tutors are rarely referred to in evaluation reports. Like Boquet, Grimm (2003) wrote about the need to pay closer attention to what happens between tutor and student—and then to share those stories with others.

> If the writing center mission were clearly focused *on what we do with and for and because of students*, then writing center research would bring this knowledge gained from interactions with students to the attention of faculty in local situations, such as faculty development workshops, as well as in more global contexts, such as publications. . . . (emphasis added, p. 43)

. . . and state report cards. Writing center research should be brought to the attention of policymakers. By failing to mention to auditors and administrators how writing centers positively engage literacy education efforts in schools, we devalue the work of teachers and students who run them, use them, and benefit from them.

In their book that describes the writing center as a community of practice, Geller, Eodice, Condon, Carroll, and Bouquet (2007) called for a more critical, collaborative, and reflective approach to writing center evaluation. They "wonder what message our neatly packaged data-bytes send about how we believe our work, the work of the writing center tutors, and the work of student writers is—or should be—valued" (pp. 123–124). When the methods we use to evaluate our writing centers fail to fully describe the work done in our centers, we fail to describe the degree to which our centers deliver on their promises, fail to show how teachers and students benefit, and fail to describe teachers' and students' agency in their own success. We misrepresent our colleagues, our tutors, and our students, and that misrepresentation can cause a considerable amount of damage. Moss (1998) reminds us that conclusions drawn from assessments are often internalized by those assessed. Writing center evaluation is a form of assessment. If we connect the assertions of writing center scholars to those of Hillocks (2002), Huot (2002, 2007), Moss (1998), and other assessment experts, we should see how important it is that we use evaluation carefully. When we add Yancey's vision for writing centers, we should see that in order to create *with* and *for* students a center to which they will return throughout their years at the high school, we must create *with* and *for* teachers and students an evaluation process that helps us do so.

> To build the kind of writing center that serves the literacy needs of 21st-century students, writing center directors must reposition their centers as *leaders* rather than leading *supporters* of literacy education.

Becoming agents in our schools' literacy efforts means that we writing center directors must become literate in our writing center's efficacy. We need to compute less and listen more, search beyond the statistics, and turn to the people for whom our centers exist. We must embrace both support and scrutiny when we ask others what they see, what they think, and what they need. We need more stories, gathered through collaborative research projects—literacy acts in themselves—that bring together the voices of members from across the school community who exhibit degrees of expertise in multiple literacies and diversity in linguistic, racial, and cultural backgrounds.

THE WRITING CENTER AS
A RESEARCH-PROVEN METHOD

In 2007, Joanne Yatvin, former president of NCTE, encouraged teachers to join with others to subvert the research-proven paradigm that has a stranglehold on teachers' and students' lives in the classroom. I think writing center directors can play a key role in this subversion. Call it subversive activism, or using our own systematic, process-approach to research to afford ourselves our own "research-proven" status, if only unofficially. The first order of defense, as Yatvin suggested, is to be able to point to the theoretical foundations of what we do. Writing center work is no different. The writing center director who becomes familiar with available scholarship from the writing center fields and any of its sister fields (assessment, composition, and ESL education, to name a few) will be one step closer to ensuring that their center's philosophy and pedagogy is firmly grounded in proven theory. Aligning mission with pedagogy and with evaluation better prepares directors to answer any questions posed about the critical role the writing center plays in the school's literacy efforts.

Lerner (2003) noted the need for assessment that aligns more closely with the goals and values of our writing centers. Having written extensively on writing center evaluation, Lerner argued that tracking student usage does not delve deeply enough into the degree to which writing centers deliver on their goal to remain student-centered. If one goal is to be student-centered, he contended, then assessment should go beyond objectifiable usage facts to include the identification of students' needs, their reasons for using or not using the writing center, the learning processes that emerge during a writing center session, and whether sessions over time help students improve as writers.

Lerner also acknowledged that the writing center's "goals themselves can often be broadened to include not just our effect on student writers, but our effect on the entire institution" (2008, p. 3). High school writing centers are particularly poised to do this. School accreditation and literacy education are institutional goals to which the writing center contributes. To determine the extent of the writing center's engagement in these efforts, the director needs to ask a lot of questions—and the right ones.

ESSENTIAL QUESTIONS FOR
WRITING CENTER EVALUATION

Initially, writing center directors need to ask themselves if their center is delivering on its promises. Those promises are conveyed through the writing center's mission, guiding philosophy, and stated core values. But to build the kind of writing center that serves the literacy needs of 21st-century students, writing center directors must also reposition their centers as *leaders* rather than leading *supporters* of literacy education. That conceptual shift alone will make a difference in the questions asked during the evaluation process. To devise a list of essential questions, writing center directors must also look to what they and experts know about adolescent literacy, about writing instruction, and about writing center work. When writing center directors can show how their center's work stacks up against what the experts say about teaching and learning, they legitimize their work, allowing them to add another notch to their "research-proven" belts.

Questions That Stem from Core Values

The writing center's mission and guiding philosophy are a good place to start when developing an assessment framework (Lerner, 2008). For example, questions can be tailored to the writing center's core values, as well as institutional goals to which the writing center contributes. Working with the mission and guiding philosophy of my writing center, I developed questions around several common core values: literacy education, serving the special needs of students, faculty development, and student achievement/school improvement. I include several sample questions here that can be folded into the collaborative research projects provided in Appendix D. The questions are easily adaptable for use in evaluating literacy centers as well.

Core Value—Writing Center as Literacy Leader:

- In what ways has the writing center acted as a change agent in the school community with regard to 1) how literacy is conceived; and 2) how literacy instruction and assessment have changed?
- To what extent does the center demonstrate commitment to serving the literacy needs of the school community: reading, writing, multimedia?
- What steps were taken through the writing center's work to learn about students' multiple literacies, including those they bring from communities outside school? What specific steps were taken to incorporate those literacies into the school's literacy education and culture?
- How were the following celebrated this year: 1) students' literacy lives and successes; 2) teachers' literacy lives; 3) families' literacy histories?

Core Value—Ensuring Our Pedagogy Serves the Specific Needs of Students:

- Do tutor selection, training, and practice reflect the writing center's mission to serve all students, including students from diverse populations and students with disabilities?
- Does our tutoring staff mirror the student body's diversity?
- What steps has the writing center taken to better serve students' multiple literacies? Students who are speakers of other languages? Students with learning disabilities? Students reading or writing below grade level?
- What changes were made to the writing center's services that emerged from students' feedback this year? What effects have been noted? How will we track the effects of those changes in the coming year?

Core Value—Teacher Professional Development/Collegiality:

- How did work in the center lead to collaborations among colleagues?
- What new discoveries about writing instruction emerged among faculty as a result of their contact with the writing center or collaborations with colleagues?
- How did we include students and colleagues in evaluating our writing center this year?
- What activities, information, or feedback point to the writing center's role in helping teachers see themselves as capable teachers of writing in their discipline? Of multiple literacies in general?
- Did the writing center director, peer tutors, faculty, or other members of the community 1) attend and/or present at a writing center seminar, regional, or national conference; 2) publish; or 3) collaborate with teachers in other districts?
- Which in-service sessions or workshops did the writing center host for district personnel? Colleagues? Pre-service teachers? Teachers from other districts?

Core Value—Student Achievement and School Improvement:

- In what ways was the writing center featured as part of the school's accreditation/continuous improvement plan? What role did the director, faculty, students, and community play in that plan?
- What feedback did state auditors or other visitors share about the writing center?

- In what important ways did tutors and students say they benefited from the work they did in the writing center in core and non-core areas? In academic and other ways?
- What anecdotal evidence do we have of a relationship between student achievement and writing center visits? What plans for research do we have for exploring that relationship in the future?
- What were the tutor-led, student-initiated changes made in our writing center this year? What effects have those changes had on student achievement?
- In what ways did the school, in general, benefit from the writing center's visibility in the district? In the community (locally)? In the media? Nationally? Internationally? .

Questions About the Writing Center's Role in Literacy Education

In order for writing center directors to position their centers as literacy leaders, they may first need to clarify what literacy means in the 21st century and then develop questions for evaluation based on their understanding. No longer does "literacy education" refer to instruction in reading and writing. The National Council of Teachers of English NCTE, (2004) acknowledged that

> [a]dolescents are already reading in multiple ways when they enter secondary classrooms, using literacy as a social and political endeavor in which they engage to make meaning and act upon their worlds. Their texts range from clothing logos to music to specialty magazines to Web sites to popular and classical literature. In the classroom it is important for teachers to recognize and value the multiple literacy resources students bring to the acquisition of school literacy. (para. 4)

From that description, the following questions for evaluating the writing center's role in the school's literacy education efforts emerge:

- In what ways does the writing center showcase the literacies students bring from their homes, neighborhoods, and affinity/peer groups?
- In what ways has the writing center nurtured students' use of literacy to make meaning of and to communicate their own experiences in the communities to which they belong? To use literacy "as a social and political endeavor"?
- To what extent does the writing center host extracurricular activities to align with literacy projects in both core and non-core classes? To provide creative outlets for students to create, showcase, and celebrate their "texts"?
- In what significant ways (academic and affective) does the tutoring

process encourage students to bring lived literacies into academic work? How does tutor training and practice reinforce the value of diverse and multiple literacies?

- In what critical ways does the writing center collaborate with teachers across the disciplines to develop assignments that 1) use text and non-text examples as models; 2) allow students to reflect what they have learned through text and non-text examples; 3) employ a multi-genre approach to teaching in that discipline while training the student to master the literacy skills needed in that discipline; and 4) incorporate technology to serve teaching and learning objectives?
- To what degree does the writing center encourage teachers to demonstrate their own literacy successes related to their content area? Unrelated to their content area?

Questions Related to Serving Diverse Students' Needs

To examine how effectively their writing centers serve diverse student populations or students with disabilities, directors can consult the International Writing Center Association's (IWCA) Disabilities Statement (2006a) and Diversity Initiative (2006b). For example, the Disabilities Statement points to the writing center's responsibility to students and tutors with disabilities. Especially helpful for developing questions that guide assessment is the first section of this document, which enumerates what every writing center should do. The statement might help directors identify areas where improvements might be made to tutor training, physical space, and available materials to better serve students and tutors with learning disabilities. For example,

- What do we know about the processes students use to learn?
- Do we hire tutors with learning disabilities? How might their experiences inform tutor selection, training, pedagogy, and faculty professional development?
- How have we trained tutors to adapt their tutoring practice to accommodate the various ways students learn and process information?
- What work have we done with colleagues to increase our and others' awareness of the needs of students with disabilities?
- In what ways do our physical space, handouts, and other materials deny access to students with learning disabilities?

Questions that may arise from the IWCA's Diversity Initiative should focus on the center's inclusivity and celebration of diversity. The Diversity Initiative describes writing centers as inherently multicultural and multilingual sites that welcome and accommodate diversity. Writing centers inclusively serve all students, including members of underrepresented groups such as people of color, lesbian, gay, bisexual, and transgender people, and people with a range of abilities, economic needs, and linguistic expression. Writing center work is also conducted by a diverse population of tutors and administrators. (para. 1)

When we evaluate our centers for how they serve diverse groups of students, we might ask:

- How does our pedagogy reflect current research in second language teaching and acquisition?
- How do we define "best practices" for use with diverse student populations, and what are they? How do we know that they work and with whom?
- What professional development efforts help prepare faculty to use those best practices?
- How many English Language Learners (ELLs) does our school serve? What languages do they speak? Do we have tutors who are speakers of other languages? How are our tutors trained to help ELLs?
- What activities does the writing center host to celebrate linguistic, ethnic, racial, and cultural diversity? How many of those activities take place during the school day? After school? Throughout the school year? To what extent do these activities invite home/lived literacies and languages?
- How have we trained tutors to adapt their tutoring practice to accommodate students' diverse cultural backgrounds? To respond to points of view and life experiences that are unlike theirs (political, religious, and otherwise)?

Summarizing the Writing Center's Success

Once all the questions are asked, it is helpful to organize the answers to identify strengths and to target areas for improvement in the coming year. For instance,

- What stories from community members give us a glimpse into what we are doing well? What might we do better?
- What stories point to ways our writing center has fostered interdependence among members of the school community?
- What characteristics might we ascribe to our center's "personality"? To what extent do those characteristics reflect our center's core

values? Which of those characteristics do we currently project to the school community?

- In what ways do short- and long-range plans reflect the center's philosophy?
- If we were to choose five of our best features to highlight in the coming year, what would they be, and how might we present them to the school community?
- Whom might we recognize from across the school community for their professional, personal, and academic successes?
- How might we need to change the assessment process next year?

FINAL THOUGHTS

The sample questions included in this chapter and the collaborative research projects I propose in Appendix D call for looking at writing center work through different and wider lenses. They hint at what we might learn about our work and how we might better advocate for teachers and students when we move away from those "voiceless texts" (Bruner, 1990) that not only fail to tell the story of the center but tell another story entirely. The stories we shared each year with auditors would never have been told if I'd stuck to a "voiceless" report form. The value of our achievements belonged to our students, our peer tutors, our faculty, and our community members. They deserved more attention than to be boiled down to a data point and tossed into a file cabinet. The unexpected outcomes of our work pointed to something much bigger under way, something systemic, something that could be seen in the students' writing, in teachers' interactions with one another, and in the way the community came together to change the way others saw the school.

Bruffee (2008) called that "something" interdependence—the most essential but unsung outcome of the writing center conference. He asserted that in each writing center conference, tutor and writer practice the "craft and essential characteristics of human interdependence" (p. 8), noting how interdependence is hard to achieve, especially "among people who don't recognize each other and who see each other as strangers" (p. 8). Race and class might have divided our school to an extent, but it was a federal law that labeled us as failures and cut us off from much of the community that surrounded us. Our district's struggles were often the topic of heated conversations around the community, where angry residents often laid more blame than they offered solutions for declining achievement, and where they closed their doors in my face and the faces of other volunteers who canvassed their neighborhoods, trying to gain support for tax levies and bond issues.

In a school such as ours, where community support was hard to come by, where test scores and other benchmark data could have determined our fate, it was easy to internalize those labels placed upon us. But we didn't. After 3 years of trying to prove that ours was not a *failing* school, we were taken off the list of schools of concern. The auditors could not deny the collaborative work they witnessed in our writing center, nor its effects on teachers, students, and community members. Our center was noted for having played an integral part in our school's accreditation status. Though our "research-proven" designation was unofficial, we certainly earned it. And you can, too.

REFERENCES

Boquet, E. (2002). *Noise from the writing center.* Logan, UT: Utah State University Press.

Bruffee, K. (2008). What being a writing peer tutor can do for you. *The Writing Center Journal, 28*(2), 5–10.

Bruner, J. (1990). *Acts of meaning.* Cambridge, MA: Harvard University Press.

Fels, D. (2008). Writing groups for teachers: Opportunities for imagination, creativity, and renewal. In K. Dvorak & S. Bruce (Eds.), *Creative approaches to writing center work* (pp. 275–298). Creskill, NJ: Hampton Press.

Geller, A., Eodice, M., Condon, F., Carroll, M., & Boquet, E. (2007). *The everyday writing center: A community of practice.* Logan, UT: Utah State University Press.

Grimm, N. (2003). In the spirit of service: Making writing center research a "featured character." In M. Pemberton & J. Kinkead (Eds.), *The center will hold* (pp. 41–57). Logan, UT: Utah State University Press.

Hillocks, G. (2002). *The testing trap: How state writing assessments control learning.* New York: Teachers College Press.

Huot, B. (2002). *(Re)articulating writing assessment for teaching and learning.* Logan, UT: Utah State Press.

Huot, B. (2007). Consistently inconsistent: Business and the Spellings Commission Report on Higher Education. *College English 69*(5), 512–525.

International Writing Centers Association. (2006a). *Position statement on disability and writing centers.* Retrieved from http://writingcenters.org/wpcontent/uploads/2008/6/disabilitiesstatement1.pdf

International Writing Centers Association. (2006b). *IWCA diversity initiative.* Retrieved from http://writingcenters.org/wpcontent/uploads/2008/06/iwca_diversity_initiative1.pdf

Lerner, N. (2003). Writing center assessment: Searching for the "proof" of our effectiveness. In M. Pemberton & J. Kinkead (Eds.), *The center will hold* (pp. 58–73). Logan, UT: Utah State University Press.

Lerner, N. (July 2008). *A framework for research on writing center effects.* Workshop presented at the 6th Annual Summer Institute for Writing Center Directors, University of Wisconsin–Madison, Madison, WI.

Moss, P. (1998). The role of consequences in validity theory. *Educational Measurement: Issues and Practice, 17*(2), 6–12.

National Council of Teachers of English. (2004). *A call to action: What we know about adolescent literacy and ways to support teachers in meeting students' needs.* Retrieved from http://www.ncte.org/positions/statements/adolescentliteracy?source=gs

Smyth, T. S. (2008). Who is No Child Left Behind leaving behind? *Clearing House, 81*(3), 133–137.

Villanueva, V. (2006). Blind: Talking about the new racism. *The Writing Center Journal, 26*(1), 3–19.

Yancey, K. B. (Speaker/Author). (2007, October). (Digital video recording). *Composition, circulation, space, and the work of writing centers.* Plenary address presented at the 2007 Regional Conference of the Midwest Writing Centers Association, Kansas City, KS. Retrieved from http://mwca07.pbwiki.com/mwca07confpro

Yatvin, J. (2007). Talking politics: Where is American education headed? *The Council Chronicle, 16*(3), 19.

Tutor Recommendation Form

Tutor Recommendations for 2010-2011

Teacher Name _____

Department _____

☐ **I do not have any students to recommend**

☐ **I have students to recommend and have listed them on the back of this document**

Colleagues,   March 3, 2010

The Literacy Center needs to start thinking about student tutor recruitment for next year. In doing so, we rely heavily on your recommendations. We are asking you to only recommend students who will be **sophomores, juniors or seniors** next year.

Please recommend your best students who:

- are **outstanding** leaders in our school community
  - work well with others
  - are friendly, patient, & reliable
  - care about the condition of their school
  - notice problems & suggest solutions!

- have both academic and personal **integrity**
- can **think critically**
- are *excellent* writers
- are *excellent* mathematicians and problem solvers
- are *excellent* readers

- remember to recommend only those students who would be **capable of tutoring any of the other students** that you teach
- decide which of your students you would like to recommend
  - help yourself make this decision by **using your portal to obtain transcripts** of the students that you teach
- list all of the students who you are recommending in the provided space on the back of this document
- jot down a few descriptive words about each student that led you to recommend him/her
- turn this document in to your **department Literacy Center Staff member** or to **Andrew Jeter by March 17th**.

Thank you so much for your support. You are essential to the Literacy Center's continued success.

If you have any questions or concerns, do not hesitate to call your department Literacy Center Staff member or Andrew Jeter, the Literacy Center Coordinator (x2615).

131

Recommended Students:

Use this table to list students who will be sophomores, juniors, or seniors next year:

	Name:	Student ID#:	Comments:
1			
2			
3			
4			
5			
6			
7			
8			
9			
10			
11			
12			
13			
14			
15			
16			
17			
18			
19			
20			

Tutor Interview Form

THE LITERACY CENTER
niles west high school

INTERVIEWER:_____ DATE:_____

INTERVIEWEE:_____ ID#:_____

IN-COMING: SOPHOMORE   JUNIOR   SENIOR

Please determine the following:

	Completed Course Work (Class/Teacher)	Planned Course Work
AS&T:		
English/ELL:		
Foreign Lang:		
Math:		
Science:		
S. Studies:		
Languages Spoken at Home:		

1. Have you ever been a tutee in the Literacy Center? Yes_____ No_____

    a. In not, why haven't you visited and what do you think the Literacy Center is about?

    b. If so, then share your experience with me. What were some positive and negative aspects of the experience?

2. What assets do you feel you can contribute to the Literacy Center?

    a. What subjects would you feel most comfortable tutoring? Explain your experience in that subject.

    b. Is there any way the Literacy Center could serve you or other students better or more effectively?

3. Have you ever tutored someone before?
    Yes   _____ (Have the interviewee describe how he/she was able to help.)
    No   _____

4. Tell us about a volunteer opportunity or a charitable event you have participated in.

5. How might you help a student who/with:

is a reluctant tutee?	is an unorganized tutee?	is a non-serious tutee?
a math problem? $2x + 3y = 1$ $-x + y = -3$	reading Shakespeare?	a German speech?
an English paper (e.g.: CEW, crafting a thesis, organizing, brainstorming)?	a global studies reading?	writing a poem?
solving a Rubik's Cube?	explaining an assignment/brainstorming?	interpreting the data from an experiment?

6. If your friend(s) come in for help and ask for you, should you work with them? Why or why not?

7. There will be an all-day training of tutors on Friday, August 20, 2010. Will you be able to attend? Yes _____ No _____

Recommendation Comments _____

Tutor Contract

TUTOR CONTRACT 2010-2011

ARTICLE I – TUTOR BEHAVIOR AND ATTITUDES
- Tutors are expected to
  - represent themselves as student-leaders in the Literacy Center, in classes, and around the school.
  - give up their free time to tutor walk-in tutees.
  - treat every tutee with respect.
  - help to maintain a safe, friendly environment that is conducive to learning.
  - use appropriate language at all times.
  - be aware of the importance of good public relations and avoid talking negatively about or disagreeing with a teacher's instructions, advice, grades, etc.
  - be aware of all announcements posted on the Tutor Board.

ARTICLES II – CONFIDENTIALITY
- Tutors are aware of the importance of confidentiality and do not discuss with other students information about the tutoring sessions in which they have participated.

ARTICLE III – ATTENDANCE
- Tutors are expected to
  - be in the Literacy Center to tutor walk-in tutees a minimum of 3 days a week.
  - be on time to all of their assigned periods or to have a pass explaining any accrued tardiness.
  - understand that the Literacy Center is not a study hall alternative or a place to work with their friends on their own work.
  - attend tutor meetings when called.
  - attend all tutor training sessions including a one day session before the start of the school year (Friday, August 20, 2010).

ARTICLE IV – ACADEMIC RESPONSIBILITY & HONESTY
- Tutors know that
  - satisfactory academic progress must be maintained with no quarter grades of D or F.
  - academic progress will be monitored throughout the year.
  - academic dishonesty will not be tolerated and will result in dismissal from the Literacy Center tutor staff.

ARTICLE V – COMMITMENT AND CREDIT
- Tutors agree to
  - a year long commitment.
  - perform the tasks required of a tutor in order to earn one full elective credit for one year of service (1/2 credit per semester).
  - engage in four Structured Conversations a year as determined by the Staff.

With my signature below, I agree to abide by the standards and expectations of the Literacy Center.

Signature	Name (Please Print)	Date

Teachers and Students as Researchers: Literacy-based, Collaborative Projects for Writing Center Evaluation

The following table details a number of collaborative research methods for evaluating a writing center, with a particular emphasis on what writing center staff can do to better advocate for teachers and students.

Appendix D: Table of Literacy-Based, Collaborative Research Projects for Writing Center Evaluation

Method	Purpose	Investigators	Task
Focus Groups	To seek answers from students about the writing center's services and what they need it to do.	Team of students	Investigators develop the questions asked, interpret the answers, and report on the findings.
Faculty Survey	To gauge faculty's use/non-use of the writing center, as well as to solicit recommendations for expanding the writing center's services to meet the needs of teachers.	Team comprised of equal numbers of supporters and critics drawn from the faculty	Investigators share their perceptions of what the writing center is doing right, as well as what could be improved. They develop questions that show how the center might be used for practical to ideal purposes.
Interviews	To gain information from faculty as to how they use multiple literacies in their classrooms, including but not limited to writing. -or- To clarify notions of literacy, "good writing," how writing is/should be taught. -or- To clarify faculty and administrative expectations for the writing center: for example, its role in literacy/writing instruction.	Team of colleagues from across the disciplines	Investigators share their department's and individual teachers' perspectives on how students' multiple literacies provide a foundation for teaching and learning in their classrooms. Investigators focus their conversations on clarification of the concepts of literacy, "good writing," and the role the writing center plays or should play in teaching.
Narratives/Service Learning	To gather insight from students on their perceptions of achievement and its relationship to tutoring sessions.	Team of self-identifying repeat users of the writing center interested in service-learning credit	Investigators gather narratives from students who feel they improved their writing (or other literacies) as a result of the work they did in the center. They identify common themes across the narratives.
Cultural Interviews	To explore the literacy lives of students and their families outside of school.	Conversation partners (students and their family members), with students playing the role of the primary investigator	Investigators ask family members to speak openly about their literacy histories, including but not limited to the effects of their education and linguistic backgrounds on their current literacy habits at home, at work, and in their community.
Observation	To identify the literacies inherent in events important to students' lives and how those practices influence the value students and their families place on literacy. -or- To gather visual illustrations of literacy as it is lived.	Team of students, parents, caregivers, and community members	Investigators observe events that occur frequently in their lives and list the acts of literacy performed in each. Pictures of literacy acts/events become exhibits throughout the school community.

Words of Wisdom from Writing Center Educators

Jill Adams, Metropolitan State College of Denver

Don't by limited by what others have done. Use that knowledge as a spring-board into what will work for your students and school. It's okay to think outside of the box in order to make things happen. Stay focused on your "field of dreams" vision, for it will carry you through when you face obstacles.

Hannah Baran, Louisa County High School

Build widespread awareness of and support for the writing center. Arrange for your student-tutors to give presentations about the writing center to each department in the school and assist the teachers in brainstorming ways they might use the center. Select a liaison from each department to promote the WC among their colleagues. Find ways to inform and involve parents in the work of the writing center. Collect and publicize positive feedback from your clients. Convince your local newspaper to run a story and invite local businesses to become sponsors. Invite your superintendent, school board members, and other local politicians to observe tutoring sessions in action. Avoid adopting an embattled mentality, but remember that even strong programs aren't impervious to budget cuts; continuously advocate for the importance of your center.

Cynthia Dean, University of Maine–Augusta

Build relationships with administration and teachers. If administration does not support the writing center, one will not get far. If teachers do not under-stand the function of or benefits associated with writing centers, it will be difficult to attract students.

Kevin Dvorak, Nova Southeastern University

If you are starting a new center, make sure to hire the most talented, motivated juniors and seniors you can find. But, more important, make sure to involve a few amazing freshmen and sophomores. Get them involved in any way you can. Empower them. They will be with you for your first few years, and, by the time they are seniors, they will have 3 or 4 years of experience at the center. They will know all the ins and outs of your center, and they will help recruit even more talented people. It's one of the most sustainable practices I have found in my time as a director.

Jon-Carlos Evans, Filmmaker

For writers and writing tutors alike—Write. Read. Think. Write. Read. Think. Ask Questions. Once your hands and eyes start to burn, take a break . . . and then, keep writing.

Dawn Fels, George Mason University

Don't give up. Remember that you are doing this exhausting work (and it is exhausting work) for the students. Realize that you may need to start with nothing. Most of us do. You may even find yourself doing this work alone. Many of us do. Enlist the help of as many colleagues, students, and community members as you can. And then protect what you build together. Keep learning. Keep expanding. Keep pushing.

Andrew Jeter, Niles West High School

When we first set out to build our literacy center, we knew that it must be open to all, volunteer-based, non-evaluative, and evolving. We also believed that it should not be personality-driven.

I have since learned that this last belief was wrong. Centers are very much driven by the personalities that run them. They are too personal a space for it to be otherwise. And this is an important consideration when deciding who in your school community will be placed at the reins of your program. Who will do whatever it takes to make the center a thriving and engaging place?

Is he or she excited about working collaboratively? Is he or she willing to walk around school all day in a Godzilla outfit? Is he or she able and willing to advance others? Is he or she willing to use a slip-n-slide to train tutors? Is he or she the person who could make school fun?

My advice: Find the person in your school who wants to make it a place where kids love to be, who will think about school from a completely different perspective, and who will put his or her ego on a shelf at the beginning of each day.

Kerri Mulqueen, Nazareth Regional High School

Don't get hung up on the idea that your writing center should be a perfect emulation of any other writing center you may have been involved with or that you may be using as a model. Every writing center is unique to its home institution and your best bet is to start looking right away for ways you can marry the mission of your writing center to the culture and activities of your school. If that means farming your peer tutors out to support classroom writing workshops, do it. If it means running writing contests through your center, do that. And by all means, cultivate relationships with teachers and guidance counselors because they are the conduit to students and an invaluable link in matching trained peer tutors with the students who can best benefit from their help.

Katherine Palacio, Monsignor Edward Pace High School

Not everything has to be perfectly planned. You will hit several bumps along the way, you will lack support at times, and you will question what you got yourself into. But when you witness frustrated students' faces changing into smiles of relief, you will know that it was all worth it in the end because helping students is what the writing center should be all about.

Ben Rafoth, Indiana University of Pennsylvania

The best advice I can give to someone who wants to open a new writing center at their institution is to get the highest-level administrator in your institution to support the concept. It's not even critical, at first, to get the funding or space nailed down, although it helps. Commitment to the idea from the top is the first step. Once you have this, you can use your relationships with others to implement what you and your principal or dean want to achieve. If the commitment is not forthcoming, don't give up. Keep working at the grassroots level, build support, and try again. Eventually, the strength of your idea will win over the skeptics because a writing center, if it is anything, is a great idea.

Justin Schulz, Musician

The first priority is to know one's tutees, their values and interests. Common ground is fertile ground. Aside from the obvious benefit of building rapport, a writing coach can learn useful insights into the tutee's motivations and limits. Coaches may more easily lead the students to their own conclusions when they understand what inspires their tutees. Although the coach wants to push the student to do better, one should be sensitive to their comfort level. Even objective criticism can incite students and put them on the defense. They may become defensive and closed to your suggestions. Alternatively, they may become insecure and afraid to share their ideas, relying on the "expert" coach to tell them what to do. Finally, the coaching session should be a lot more enjoyable for the tutor when he or she has shared interest with the tutee.

Jennifer Wells, Florida State University

No matter what else happens, focus on the little moments that happen in the center, moments that, if you aren't paying attention, you'll miss. Focus on the beam of a student who finally understands what a thesis sentence is. Focus on the patience you see your peer tutors exhibit, patience that often you don't even have. Focus on the silliness, the laughter, the deep sigh of a space that is unlike any other on campus. These are why you do the work you do, and these are what make it possible to keep going, even in the face of uncertain odds.

About the Contributors

Jill Adams is an assistant professor of English at Metropolitan State College of Denver. She teaches Composition 1010, Young Adult Literature, and Teaching Composition 7–12.

Hannah Baran grew up in Orlando and Boston. She became a peer tutor at Lake Highland Prep and later tutored varsity athletes at the University of Virginia, where she graduated with degrees in American Studies and English Education. She continues to live in central Virginia with her husband and two dogs. Hannah currently teaches upperclassmen at Louisa County High School, where she helped to found the region's only secondary writing center in 2011. She enjoys crossword puzzles, chocolate, and sailing. She can be contacted via Facebook.

Cynthia Dean is an assistant professor of Education and coordinator of teacher certification at the University of Maine at Augusta. Actively involved in the Maine Writing Project, she is the coordinator of the MWP's annual Maine High School Writing Centers conference. She and her husband recently built their dream house in Liberty, Maine, where they live life as simply as possible with their German Shepherd, two cats, and eight chickens.

Kevin Dvorak is an associate professor and writing center and WAC coordinator at Nova Southeastern University. He is also the president of the Southeastern Writing Centers Association. His first book, *Creative Approaches to Writing Center Work*, was co-edited with Shanti Bruce and won the 2008 IWCA Outstanding Scholarship Award. He has also published in the award-winning *ESL Writers: A Guide for Writing Center Tutors, The Writing Center Director's Resource Book, Praxis, The Writing Center Journal, Southern Discourse*, and *The Dangling Modifier*.

Jon-Carlos Evans is a New York–based writer/director, VJ, and multimedia artist born in St. Louis, Missouri. After graduating from University City High School, he received a B.A. in Film Production from Webster University. His senior thesis, *Salvation (Without You)*, was awarded the Eastman Kodak Student Grant and screened in the 2006 St. Louis Filmmakers Showcase. After relocating to New York City in 2007, his films *Julya, Smile,* and *From New York* went on to screen as a part of the 32nd Asian-American International Film Festival in New York and the 2nd Edition of the International Streaming Festival for Audiovisual Art in the Netherlands. In 2009, Evans completed his MFA at the City College of New York in Media Arts Production. His most recent short film, *Antithesis,* has recently been honored by the 2010 Honolulu International Film Festival's Aloha Accolade Award for Excellence and the Silver Palm Award at the 2010 Mexico International Film Festival, among others. He resides in New York City, where he works as a freelance director, editor, and cinematographer.

Dawn Fels teaches composition and directs The Writing Center at George Mason University. As a high school English teacher, Fels started a writing center in an urban-suburban high school placed on corrective action. Her experiences there started her on a research agenda that examines the effects of federal and state curricular policies on teachers and students and the role of writing centers in school improvement plans and school reform. A loyal St. Louis Cardinals fan, Fels once planned a writing center conference in St. Louis during the week she anticipated the Cardinals would win the World Series. They did.

Andrew Jeter is a founder and the coordinator of the Literacy Center at Niles West High School in Skokie, Illinois. Since his center opened in 2005, he has educated more than 900 tutors. He is the co-founder of the Chicagoland Organization of Writing, Literacy, and Learning Centers, which represents more than 40 secondary schools. Andrew is currently a Ph.D. candidate in Composition at Indiana University of Pennsylvania. He also enjoys frozen sheet cake.

Kerri Mulqueen is a doctoral candidate in the English Department at St. John's University in Queens, New York, and the chairperson of the English Department at Nazareth Regional High School in Brooklyn, New York. Her research interests center around secondary writing centers and urban education. A passionate teacher, Mets fan, and newly converted vegetarian, she lives in Queens with her husband, Nick Baldassaro, and their many pets.

Katherine Palacio is a teacher at a private high school in Miami. She received her B.A. in English Literature from Florida International University in 2005 and her M.A. in Writing from Nova Southeastern University in 2010. She manages the writing center at her high school, which is staffed by St. Thomas University students under the direction of Kevin Dvorak, and she writes frequently for *The Miami Laker,* a community newspaper.

Ben Rafoth has directed the Writing Center at Indiana University of Pennsylvania for 23 years. He teaches undergraduate courses in writing and editing and graduate courses in composition and TESOL. Ben received IWCA's Book of the Year Award (with Shanti Bruce) for *ESL Writers* and NCPTW's Ron Maxwell Award for Distinguished Leadership. He edited *A Tutor's Guide*, 2nd edition, and served on the executive board of the IWCA. He chaired the first joint conference of IWCA and NCPTW in 2003 and was a Summer Institute leader in 2005 and again in 2010.

Justin Schulz, ENTP, Composer/Barista. Likes comic books and bicycling. Born in St. Louis. Lives in New York. Writing Coach at University City High School and Webster University, St Louis.

Jennifer Wells was the reading and writing specialist at Mercy High School in Burlingame, California, from 2004–2011, and is now the director of The Reading-Writing Center at Florida State University. She recently concluded a longitudinal study of the literacy knowledge that high school students are able to transfer to college. In her free time, she can be found in the rainforests of Borneo, the savannas of Tanzania, or the souks of Morocco.

Index